International English

International English

A guide to varieties of Standard English

Third edition

Peter Trudgill and Jean Hannah

Edward Arnold
A member of the Hodder Headline Group
LONDON NEW YORK SYDNEY AUCKLAND

Edward Arnold is a division of Hodder Headline PLC
338 Euston Road, London NW1 3BH

© 1982, 1985, 1994 Peter Trudgill and Jean Hannah

First published in the United Kingdom 1982
Third edition 1994

8 7 6 5 4 3 2
99 98 97 96 95

Distributed exclusively in the USA by St Martin's Press Inc.
175 Fifth Avenue, New York, NY 10010, USA

British Library Cataloguing in Publication Data
Trudgill, Peter
International English: Guide to Varieties of Standard English. - 3Rev.ed
I. Title   II. Hannah, Jean
427

ISBN 0-340-58645-1

**This book is accompanied by a recording which is available on
cassette only**

Typeset by Wearset, Boldon, Tyne and Wear
Printed and bound in the United Kingdom by
J W Arrowsmith Ltd, Bristol

For Mum, Dad and Mom

Note to the third edition

This third edition has benefited from corrections, additional information and suggestions kindly provided by reviewers and by many correspondents. It has also, we hope, been improved as a consequence of updating and expansion which resulted from further studies made by the authors in New Zealand and the British Isles. The years since the publication of the first and second editions have seen a continued growth in publication on and interest in varieties of English around the world; this development is reflected in the additional information contained in this substantially revised version of the text, as well as in an updated Further reading section.

Peter Trudgill
Jean Hannah
January 1993

Acknowledgements

Very many people have helped with the writing of this book, by supplying information, reading and correcting earlier versions of the typescript, and by advising on content and format. We cannot list them all, but are grateful to all of them. We would particularly like to thank the following: J. Allwood, L. Bauer, A. Bell, J. Bernard, K. Bhat, C. Biggs, J. K. Chambers, J. Clark, A. Davison, J. A. Edmondson, J. R. Edwards, V. K. Edwards, S. Foldvik, E. Gordon, C. W. Kisseberth, Bh. Krishnamurti, L. Lanham, S. Millar, J. Milroy, J. L. Morgan, S. N. Sridhar, D. Sutcliffe, A. R. Thomas, J. Ure, S. K. Verma and J. C. Wells. We are also very grateful to colleagues in the Department of Linguistic Science of Reading University, who helped in many ways.

Contents

Symbols

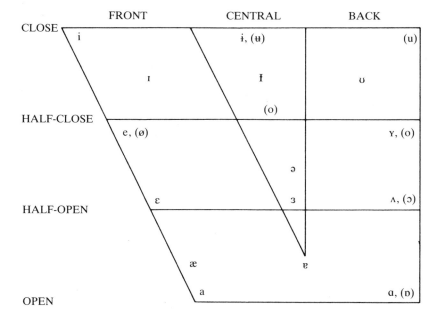

General symbols

[ ] — phonetic transcription (indicates actual pronunciation)
/ / — phonemic transcription
~ — 'alternates with'
* — indicates ungrammatical sentence
? — indicates sentence of questionable grammaticality

English vowel symbols

A vowel can be described by its position on two dimensions: *open* vs *close*, and *front* vs *back*. This position corresponds roughly to the position in the mouth of the highest point of the tongue in the production of that vowel. Presence of lip rounding is indicated on the diagram opposite by parentheses.

Diacritics

т   more open
ⵑ   more back
⊥   more close
⊣   more front
:   long
·   half-long
ʹ   stress

English consonant phonemes

/p/	as	*p*	in	*peat*
/t/	as	*t*	in	*treat*
/č/	as	*ch*	in	*cheat*
/k/	as	*k*	in	*kite*
/b/	as	*b*	in	*bite*
/d/	as	*d*	in	*date*
/ǰ/	as	*j*	in	*jute*
/g/	as	*g*	in	*gate*
/f/	as	*f*	in	*fate*
/θ/	as	*th*	in	*thought*
/s/	as	*s*	in	*site*
/š/	as	*sh*	in	*sheet*
/h/	as	*h*	in	*hate*
/v/	as	*v*	in	*vote*
/ð/	as	*th*	in	*that*
/z/	as	*z*	in	*zoo*
/ž/	as	*s*	in	*vision*
/l/	as	*l*	in	*late*
/r/	as	*r*	in	*rate*
/w/	as	*w*	in	*wait*
/j/	as	*y*	in	*yet*
/m/	as	*m*	in	*meet*
/n/	as	*n*	in	*neat*
/ŋ/	as	*ng*	in	*long*

Other consonant symbols

[ʔ]	glottal stop
[ł]	velarized or 'dark' *l*, as in RP *all*
[ɬ]	voiceless lateral fricative
[ɹ]	post-alveolar frictionless continuant, as *r* in RP *right*
[ɾ]	alveolar flap, *r* in Spanish *pero*
[ç]	voiceless palatal fricative
[x]	voiceless velar fricative, as *ch* in German *nacht*
[ɸ]	voiceless bilabial fricative
[ʍ]	voiceless *w*
[d̪]	voiced alveolar flap
C̪	dental consonant
C̢	retroflex consonant
Cʰ	aspirated consonant
C̩	syllabic consonant

1
Varieties of Standard English

The subject of this book is *Standard English*, the variety of the English language which is normally employed in writing and normally spoken by 'educated' speakers of the language. It is also, of course, the variety of English that students of English as a Foreign or Second Language (EFL/ESL) are taught when receiving formal instruction. The term *Standard English* refers to grammar and vocabulary (*dialect*) but not to pronunciation (*accent*). Thus:

I haven't got any

is a sentence of Standard English, no matter how it is pronounced, while

I ain't got none

is not a sentence of Standard English, consisting as it does of forms used in many non-standard dialects. In this book, however, we shall also be dealing with those accents of English that are normally used by speakers of Standard English and are therefore most closely associated with this variety. Note, too, that Standard English includes informal as well as formal styles:

I haven't got a bloody clue

is Standard English, while

I ain't got no idea

is not.

1.1. The two main standard varieties

Traditionally, schools and universities in Europe—and in many other parts of the world—have taught that variety of English often referred to as 'British English'. As far as grammar and vocabulary are concerned, this generally means Standard English as it is normally written and spoken by educated speakers in England and, with minor differences, in Wales, Scotland, Northern Ireland, The Republic of Ireland, Australia, New Zealand and South Africa. As far as pronunciation is concerned, it means something much more restrictive, for the RP ('Received Pronunciation') accent which is taught to foreigners is actually used by perhaps only 3–5 per cent of the population of England. The RP accent has its origins in the south-east of England but is currently a social accent associated with the BBC, the Public Schools in England, and with members of the upper-middle and upper classes. It is considered a prestigious accent in the whole of the British Isles and British Commonwealth, but it is for the most part an accent associated only with England. For this reason, in this book we shall refer to the combination of British Standard English grammar and vocabulary with the RP accent as *English* English (EngEng) rather than British English.

The other form of Standard English that is widely taught to students of EFL and ESL we shall refer to as North American English (NAmEng), meaning English as it is written and spoken by educated speakers in the United States of America and Canada. (If we wish to distinguish between these two North American varieties, we shall write United States English (USEng) and Canadian English (CanEng).) NAmEng is, naturally, taught to students learning English in North America, and also to those in many parts of Latin America and other areas of the world.

Until recently, many European universities and colleges not only taught EngEng but actually *required* it from their students; i.e. other varieties of Standard English were not allowed. This was often the result of a conscious decision that some norm needed to be established and that confusion would arise if teachers offered conflicting models. Lately, many universities have come to relax this requirement, recognizing that their students are as likely (if not more likely) to encounter NAmEng as EngEng, especially since some European students study for a time in North America. Many universities therefore now permit students to speak and write *either* EngEng *or* NAmEng, *so long as they are consistent* (or that, at least, is the theory).

We feel that this is a step in the right direction but it is also somewhat unrealistic. For example, it is not reasonable to expect a Dutch student of English who has learnt EngEng at school and then studied for a year in the USA to return to the Netherlands with anything other than some mixture of NAmEng and EngEng. This is exactly what happens to British or American native speakers who cross the Atlantic for any length of time. Given that the ideal which foreign students are aiming at is native-like competence in English, we feel there is nothing reprehensible about such a mixture and that tolerating it is by no means necessarily a bad thing. Neither is it necessarily bad or confusing for schoolchildren to be exposed to more than one model.

In any case, whatever the exact form of the requirements placed on students of English by different universities and in different countries, it is clear that exposure to and/or recognition of the legitimacy of these two varieties of Standard English in English language-learning is likely to bring with it certain problems. Both those teachers wishing to insist on a rigid use of only, say, EngEng to the exclusion of NAmEng and those wishing to permit use of both varieties need to be quite clear about which forms occur in which variety. For example, teachers of EngEng (whether they are native speakers or not) who encounter expressions such as 'First of all . . ., second of all . . .' or 'I did it in five minutes time' in a student's work are likely to regard these as typical learner's mistakes unless they are aware that these forms are perfectly normal in some varieties of NAmEng. Similarly, teachers of NAmEng may mark as incorrect certain forms which are perfectly acceptable in EngEng, such as 'I might do' and 'I'll give it him'.

Students in many parts of Asia and Africa are more likely to come into contact with Australian English (AusEng), New Zealand English (NZEng—jointly AusNZEng), or South African English (SAfEng) than with EngEng or NAmEng. It is useful for students and teachers of English in these areas, too, to be aware of the differences between their standard variety of English and the other standard varieties.

It is our hope that this book and recording will provide at least a partial solution to the problem of recognizing and coping with differences among the standard varieties of English by covering differences at the levels of phonetics, phonology, grammar and vocabulary. (Differences in intonation patterns, fine phonetic detail, and regional and non-standard varieties are not treated at length; little is known about differences in discourse features, but some remarks are included.) This information should be of assistance in particular to teachers and students of EFL. Teachers need to be aware of differences in order to present one or more standard variety clearly and to assess students' work, while non-native speakers who have learnt or are learning one variety of English should find it useful to increase their ability to understand other varieties of spoken and written Standard English. This book can also be of help to native speakers of English, for even though native speakers understand many more varieties of their language than they speak, differences in accent and subtle or unexpected differences in dialect can hamper understanding for them, too. Finally, this material should also be of interest to anyone working in English linguistics or dialectology.

1.2. The spread of English

The English language developed out of Germanic dialects that were brought to Britain, during the course of the 5th and 6th centuries, by the Jutes (from modern Jutland, Denmark), Angles (from modern Schleswig, Denmark/Germany), Saxons (from modern Holstein, Germany), and Frisians (from modern Friesland, Netherlands/Germany). By mediaeval times, this Germanic language had replaced the original Celtic language of Britain in nearly all of England as well as in southern and eastern Scotland. Until the 1600s, however, English remained a language spoken by a relatively small number of people and was confined geographically to the island of Britain. Indeed, even much of Britain remained non-English-speaking. The original Celtic language of Britain survived in the form of Welsh in nearly all of Wales and as Cornish in much of Cornwall. The Highlands and Islands of western and northern Scotland spoke Gaelic, another Celtic language which had been brought across from Ireland in pre-mediaeval times. And the populations of the Northern Isles—Orkney and Shetland—still spoke the Scandinavian language, Norn, which they had inherited from their Viking ancestors. It was not until the 17th century that the English language began the geographical and demographic expansion which was to lead to the situation in which it finds itself today, with more non-native speakers than any other language in the world, and more native speakers than any other language except Chinese.

This expansion began in the late 1600s, with the arrival of English-speakers in the Americas—North America (the modern United States and Canada), Bermuda, the Bahamas, and the Caribbean—and the importation of English, from Scotland, into the northern areas of Ireland. Subsequently, during the 1700s, English also began to penetrate into southern Ireland, and it was during this time, too, that Cornish finally disappeared from Cornwall, and Norn from Orkney and Shetland. During the 1800s, English began making serious inroads into Wales, so that today only 20 per cent of the population of that country are native Welsh-speakers; and in Scotland, English also began to replace Gaelic, which today has around 70000 native-speakers.

It was also during the 1800s that the development of Southern Hemisphere varieties of English began. During the early 19th century, large-scale colonization of Australia began to take place and, at a slightly later date, New Zealand, South Africa and the Falkland Islands also began to be colonized from the British Isles. The South Atlantic islands of St Helena and Tristan da Cunha also acquired English-speaking populations during the 1800s, as did Pitcairn Island and, subsequently, Norfolk Island in the south Pacific (see Chapter 6).

Not surprisingly, these patterns of expansion, settlement and colonization have had an effect on the relationships, similarities and differences between the varieties of English which have grown up in different parts of the world.For example, there are very many similarities between Scottish (ScotEng) and northern Irish English (NIrEng). NAmEng and the English of southern Ireland (SIrEng) also have many points of similarity. And the English varieties of the Southern Hemisphere (Australia, New Zealand, South Africa, Falklands), which were transplanted relatively recently from the British Isles, are very similar to those of the south-east of England, from where most emigrants to Australasia and South Africa came. They are quite naturally much less different from the English of England than are the varieties spoken in the Americas, which were settled much earlier. Welsh English (WEng), too, is structurally very similar to EngEng, although the influence of Welsh has played a role in its formation.

These differences and similarities are most obvious at the level of pronunciation. Varieties of English around the world differ relatively little in their consonant systems, and most differences can be observed at the level of vowel systems. Even here, differences are not enormous. The most distinctive varieties in terms of their vowel systems, however, are (a) those of Scotland and northern Ireland (see Chapter 5), and (b) those of the Caribbean. The distinctiveness of Scottish and northern Irish English reflect ancient differences between northern and southern British varieties of English, which in some cases go back to mediaeval times. The distinctiveness of the Caribbean varieties, on the other hand, reflects the influence of African languages and of the process of creolization (see Chapter 6) in their formation.

We have attempted to portray the relationships among the pronunciation of the major non-Caribbean varieties in Figure 1.1. This diagram is somewhat arbitrary and slightly misleading (there are, for example, accents of USEng which are closer to RP than to mid-western US English), but it does show the two main types of pronunciation: an 'English' type (EngEng, WEng, SAfEng, AusEng, NZEng) and an 'American' type (USEng, CanEng), with IrEng falling somewhere between the two and ScotEng being somewhat by itself.

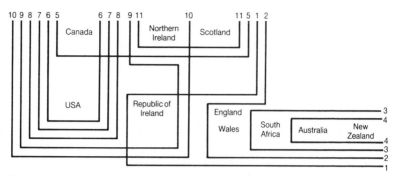

Figure 1.1.

Key

1. /ɑ:/ rather than /æ/ in *path* etc
2. absence of non-prevocalic /r/
3. close vowels for /æ/ and /ɛ/, monophthongization of /ai/ and /ɑu/
4. front [a:] for /ɑ:/ in *part* etc.
5. absence of contrast of /ɒ/ and /ɔ:/ as in *cot* and *caught*
6. /æ/ rather than /ɑ:/ in *can't* etc.
7. absence of contrast of /ɒ/ and /ɑ:/ as in *bother* and *father*
8. consistent voicing of intervocalic /t/
9. unrounded [ɑ] in *pot*
10. syllabic /r/ in *bird*
11. absence of constrast of /ʊ/ and /u:/ as in *pull* and *pool*

Lexically and grammatically, the split between the 'English' and 'American' types is somewhat neater, with USEng and CanEng being opposed on most counts to the rest of the English-speaking world. This generalization holds true in spite of the fact that each variety has its individual lexical and grammatical characteristics and that, for instance, at some points where ScotEng and IrEng grammar differ from EngEng, they closely resemble NAmEng.

The 'English' types of English, which do not differ greatly from EngEng, will be treated first in this book and are discussed in Chapter 2. The 'American' types, and the relatively larger amount of differences between them and the 'English' types, are dealt with, necessarily at greater length, in Chapters 3 and 4. ScotEng and IrEng, which we classify as neither 'English' nor 'American' types, are discussed in Chapter 5.

Of native varieties of English spoken in other areas, Bermudian English is more of the 'American' type, while the English spoken on Tristan da Cunha and the Falkland Islands are more of the 'English' type, the latter bearing some resemblances to AusEng.

English-based pidgins and creoles, which are discussed in Chapter 6, have a much more complex history than other English varieties. They include the Atlantic pidgins, creoles and pidginized varieties of the Caribbean area, the Atlantic coasts of North, Central and South America, the island of St Helena, and West Africa; and the Pacific varieties of Papua New Guinea, the Solomon Islands, and Vanuatu, among others. American Black Vernacular English also has a creole history, and there are transplanted off-shoots of it in Liberia and the Dominican Republic. There are also well-established second-language varieties of English such as those found in Africa, Malaysia and the Indian sub-continent. Chapter 7 discusses these second-language varieties.

Map No. 1. Native English-speaking areas

Australia

New
Zealand

South Africa

Liberia

St. Helena

Tristan de Cunha

Falkland Islands

Bermuda

Bahamas
Caribbean
Islands

Guyana

Canada

USA

Key for map of
British Isles

1 England
2 Scotland
3 Wales
4 Northern Ireland
5 Republic of Ireland

2
English, Australasian, South African and Welsh English

In this chapter we discuss the 'English' types of English and point out the relationships and differences between them. At certain points we also contrast and compare the 'English' types with NAmEng, but this is done in more detail in Chapters 3 and 4.

2.1. The RP accent

As we have already mentioned, the accent which is normally taught to students who are studying EngEng is the accent known as RP. This is also the accent which is described in Gimson (1990) and in most other English textbooks. There are a number of advantages to learning this particular accent. First, while it originated in the south-east of England, it is now a genuinely regionless accent within Britain; i.e. if speakers have an RP accent, you cannot tell which area of Britain they come from, which is not the case for any other type of British accent. This means that this accent is likely to be encountered and understood throughout the country. Second, RP is the accent which is used most often in radio and television broadcasts in England, so a student will have many opportunities to listen to it.

There are also disadvantages to learning only RP. First, it is an accent used natively by only 3–5 per cent of the population of England. This means that students arriving in England for the first time may have difficulty—sometimes a great deal of difficulty—understanding the other 95–97 per cent of the population. (One book which attempts to help with this problem is Hughes and Trudgill, 1987.) Second, while RP is not a regional accent, it *is* a social accent, associated particularly with the upper-middle and upper classes (and those who aspire to those classes). Foreigners who are very successful at acquiring an RP accent may therefore be reacted to as if they were upper-class—and the reaction might not *always* be favourable! Third, the RP accent is probably rather more difficult for many foreigners to acquire than, say, a Scottish accent, since RP has a large number of diphthongs and a not particularly close relationship to English orthography.

2.1.1.   The RP vowel system

Table 2.1.   The RP vowel system*

/ɪ/	*bid, very, mirror, wanted, horses, honest*
/ɛ/	*bed, merry*
/æ/	*bad, marry*
/ɒ/	*pot, long, cough, horrid*
/ʌ/	*putt, hurry*
/ʊ/	*put*
/iː/	*bee*
/ei/	*bay*
/ai/	*buy*
/ɔi/	*boy*
/uː/	*boot*
/ou/	*boat*
/ɑu/	*bout*
/ɪə/	*peer, idea*
/ɛə/	*pair, Mary*
/ʊə/	*poor*
/ɔə/	*pore*
/ɔː/	*paw, port, talk, boring*
/ɑː/	*bard, path, dance, half, banana, father, calm*
/ɜː/	*bird, furry*
/ə/	*about, sofa, butter*
/aiə/	*fire*
/ɑuə/	*tower*

**The words in Table 2.1. are also used in the recording for WIEng, WAFEng and IndEng (see page 145).*

The RP vowel system is presented in Table 2.1 above and can also be heard on the recording. While RP does not have any regional variation, as we have said, it does have variation of other types. In particular, there is variation between what some writers have called 'conservative' and 'advanced' RP (see Gimson, 1990 and Wells, 1982). For the most part this reflects linguistic changes that are currently taking place in RP, with 'conservative' pronunciations being most typical of older speakers and 'advanced' pronunciations typical of younger speakers. Some of these differences are the following:

1.   As in a number of other accents, the distinction between /ɔə/ and /ɔ:/ is now lost for very many speakers, with /ɔə/ becoming monophthongized. A more recent, but by now also wide-spread development, is the loss of /ʊə/ and the merger of this diphthong, also, with /ɔ:/. This latter change for some speakers has affected some words but not others, so that *sure* may be /šɔ:/ but *poor*, /pʊə/. The current situation with respect to these vowels is something like this:

	paw	*pore*	*poor*
older speakers	/ɔ:/	/ɔə/	/ʊə/
middle-aged speakers	/ɔ:/	/ɔ:/	/ʊə/
younger speakers	/ɔ:/	/ɔ:/	/ɔ:/

2.   There is a strong tendency, perhaps part of the same process whereby /ɔə/ > /ɔ:/, for original triphthongs formed from /ai/ and /au/ plus /ə/ to be pronounced as monophthongs, e.g. *tower* /tauə/ > /tɑ:/. This process can be labelled *smoothing* (see Wells, 1982).

3.   Where orthographic *o* occurs before the voiceless fricatives /f/, /θ/z/s/, older speakers sometimes pronounce the vowel as /ɔ:/, e.g. *off* /ɔ:f/, *froth* /frɔ:θ/, *lost* /lɔ:st/. This pronunciation is currently dying out in RP and being replaced by /ɒ/. Words like *salt* and *fault* may also be pronounced with /ɔ:/, but are often pronounced with /ɒ/, too, by younger speakers.

4.   Conservative RP has a back vowel [u:] in words like *boot*, but for younger speakers the vowel may increasingly be fronted in the direction of [ʉ:] except before /l/, as in *fool*.

5.   The diphthong /ou/ of *boat* varies considerably, ranging from [ɔʊ] among conservative speakers to [øʉ] among some advanced speakers. Perhaps the most neutral pronunciation is around [əu].

6.   The diphthong /ɛə/ of *pair* is very often monophthongized to [ɛ:] (cf. 1. and 2. above).

7.   Words like *suit* may be pronounced either /su:t/ or /sju:t/. The tendency is for middle-aged and younger speakers to omit the /j/ after /s/ before /u:/, but this tendency is much stronger in some words, e.g. *super*, *Susan*, than in others, e.g. *suit*. Word-internally, /j/ tends to be retained, as in *assume* /əsju:m/. There is also fluctuation after /l/: word-initially *lute* /lu:t/ is normal, but it is possible to pronounce, for example, *illusion* as /ɪlju:žn/.

8.   There is an increasing tendency for /ʊ/, as in *put*, to be pronounced with an unrounded vowel [ɤ].

2.1.2. Vowels in near-RP accents

Since RP speakers make up a very small percentage of the English population, many native speakers working as teachers of English are not native speakers *of RP*. If they are from the south of England, particularly the south-east, it is likely that their accents will closely *resemble* RP (especially if they are of middle-class origin), but not be identical to it. Typical differences between the RP vowel system and many near-RP south-of-England accents are the following:

1.   The /iː/ of *bee*, rather than the /ɪ/ of *bid*, occurs in the final syllable of *very*, *many*, etc. in the near-RP accents. In this respect, these accents resemble NAmEng, SAfEng and AusNZEng.

2.   The fronting of /uː/ towards [ʉː] is more widespread than in RP. Thus the allophone of /uː/ before /l/, which is not fronted in either type of accent, is, in near-RP, markedly different from those allophones that occur in all other environments. Unlike advanced RP, this variation of allophones with respect to /l/ also occurs with the diphthong /ou/. Thus:

	rude	*rule*	*code*	*coal*
Conservative RP	[ruːd]	[ruːɫ]	[koud]	[kouɫ]
Advanced RP	[rʉːd]	[ruːɫ]	[køud]	[køʉɫ]
Near-RP, southern	[rʉːd]	[ruːɫ]	[køud]	[kouɫ]

3.   The vowel /ɪ/ in unstressed syllables in RP often corresponds to /ə/ in near-RP accents. The actual distribution of /ɪ/ and /ə/ varies considerably among the different near-RP accents. By way of illustration, there are some near-RP accents which have /ɪ/ in *honest*, *village*, but /ə/ in *wanted*, *horses*. In these accents, therefore, the RP distinction between *roses* /rouzɪz/ and *Rosa's* /rouzəz/ (also found in many NAmEng accents) does not occur, both forms being /rouzəz/.

4.   Speakers with northern near-RP accents are likely to differ from RP in one important phonological respect. Like RP, they have a contrast between /æ/ and /ɑː/ as demonstrated by the following pairs:

/æ/	**/ɑː/**
pat	*part*
Pam	*palm*
match	*march*

However, there are two groups of words where RP has /ɑː/ but northern accents have /æ/. These are:

(a)   words in which RP has /ɑː/ where orthographic *a* is followed by the voiceless fricatives /f/, /θ/, or /s/: *laugh*, *path*, *grass*;

(b)   words in which RP has /ɑː/ where orthographic *a* is followed by the nasal clusters /nt/, /ns/, /nš/, /nd/ and /mp/: *plant*, *dance*, *branch*, *demand*, *sample*. (Note that southern EngEng has *branch* as /braːnš/, northern EngEng /brænč/.)

5.   Some speakers from the Midlands and north of England may have local accents which lack the vowel /ʌ/ of *putt* and *hurry*. In such accents words such as these have the vowel /ʊ/ instead, with the consequence that *but* and *put* are perfect rhymes: /bʊt/, /pʊt/.

2.1.3. RP consonants

1.   /l/. One feature of the RP accent, which it shares with many other EngEng accents and those of other 'English' varieties but is not found in NAmEng, ScotEng or IrEng, concerns the positional allophones of the consonant *l*. Syllable-initial /l/ as in *lot* is 'clear', i.e. pronounced with the body of the tongue raised towards the hard palate, giving a front vowel resonance, while syllable-final /l/ as in *hill* and syllabic /l/ as in *bottle* are 'dark' or velarized, i.e. pronounced with the body of the tongue raised towards the soft palate, giving a back-vowel resonance. Thus *lull* /lʌl/ is pronounced [lʌɫ]. (This difference also holds in AusNZEng. For NAmEng, IrEng and ScotEng, see Chapters 3 and 5.) Note that in certain non-RP south-of-England accents, [ɫ] may be considerably darker than in RP or even become vocalized, e.g. *hill* [hɪʊ].
2.   /ʍ/. Most EngEng accents have lost the original /w/:/ʍ/ contrast as in *witch*:*which*, *Wales*:*whales*. This is for the most part true also of RP, but there are some (especially older) RP speakers who still preserve it, and one suspects this is often the result of a conscious decision and effort to do so.
3.   [ʔ]. In many varieties of English in the British Isles (i.e. EngEng, NIrEng, ScotEng), the consonant /t/ may be realized as a glottal stop [ʔ], except at the beginning of a stressed syllable. This usage of the glottal stop is known technically as 'glottaling'. Thus:

top	[top]
between	[bɪtwiːn]
bitter	[bɪtə~bɪʔə]
fit	[fɪt~fɪʔ]

In RP itself the glottal stop can appear only in the following two environments:

(a)   as a realization of syllable-final /t/ before a following consonant, as in:

fit them	[fɪtðəm~fɪʔðəm]
batman	[bætmn̩~bæʔmn̩]

This is a relatively recent development in RP and is most often heard from younger speakers. It is variable in its occurrence and occurs more frequently before some consonants (e.g. /m/)

than others (e.g. /h/). In RP /t/ is *not* realized as [ʔ] between two vowels in environments such as *bitter* or *fit us*.

(b) [ʔ] occurs before /č/ and in certain consonant clusters, as in *church* [čɜːʔč], *box* [bɒʔks], *simply* [sɪmʔplɪ], where it is known as 'glottal reinforcement' or 'glottalization'.

Neither of these types of pronunciation is normally taught to foreigners, but students should be aware of them. It is probable that the occurrence of [ʔ] in words like those in (b), in particular, helps lead to the impression many North Americans have that the RP accents sounds 'clipped'; and that its absence in either environment contributes to the 'foreignness' of non-native accents.

4. /r/.

(a) As is well-known, some English accents are 'rhotic' or 'r-ful' and others are 'non-rhotic' or 'r-less'. Rhotic accents are those which actually pronounce /r/, corresponding to orthographic *r*, in words like *far* and *farm*: /faːr/, /faːrm/. The consonant *r* in these positions—word-finally before a pause, or before a consonant—is known as 'non-prevocalic /r/'. Most of south-western England, together with part of Lancashire in the north-west, have rhotic accents. Non-rhotic accents do not have /r/ in these positions and have, for example, *farm* as /faːm/. Most of southern and eastern EngEng regional accents are non-rhotic. RP is a non-rhotic accent, and thus has no contrasts of the type:

ma	*mar*
cawed	*cord*

(b) Speakers of many non-rhotic accents, while not pronouncing orthographic *r* word-finally before a pause or before a consonant, do pronounce it where there is a following word which begins with a vowel:

It's not far	no /r/
He's far behind	no /r/
She's far away	/r/ pronounced

That is to say, words like *far* have two pronunciations, depending on whether or not there is a following vowel. In non-rhotic accents, the /r/ that occurs in *far away*, etc. is known as *linking /r/*. The RP accent has this linking /r/. Failure by students to pronounce linking /r/ does not usually affect comprehension but may result in their sounding stilted or foreign. Note, however, that not all non-rhotic accents of English have linking /r/—see Table 2.2 below.

(c) As a further development, and by analogy with linking /r/,

Table 2.2. /r/

	for Non-prevocalic /r/	*for it* Linking /r/	*saw it* Intrusive /r/
RP	no	yes	variable
Non-RP, South EngEng	no	yes	yes
ScotEng	yes	—	no
IrEng	yes	—	no
CanEng	yes	—	no
Mid-West USEng	yes	—	no
Northeastern USEng	no	yes	yes
Lower Southern USEng	no	no	no
AusEng	no	yes	yes
NZEng	no	yes	yes
SAfEng	no	no	no

there are now many accents of English in which an /r/ is inserted before a following vowel even though there is no *r* in the spelling. This /r/ is known as *intrusive* /r/. In many EngEng accents it occurs in environments such as:

draw	/drɔ:/	*draw up*	/drɔ:rʌp/

on the pattern of *soar—soar up*

pa	/pɑ:/	*pa and*	/pɑ:rənd/

on the pattern of *far—far and*

China	/čainə/	*China and*	/čainərənd/

on the pattern of *finer—finer and*

idea	/aidɪə/	*idea and*	/aidɪərənd/

on the pattern of *near—near and*

It can also occur word-internally, as in *drawing* /drɔ:rɪŋ/. Obviously, what has happened historically is that the loss of /r/ before consonants in non-rhotic accents, which led to alternations of the *far—far away* type, has become reinterpreted as a rule which inserts /r/ after the vowels /ɑ:/, /ɔ:/, /ɜ:/, /ɪə/, /ɛə/ and /ə/, before a following vowel.

Does RP have intrusive /r/? Many textbooks suggest that it does not. The actual situation, however, is that today most RP speakers, particularly younger ones, do have intrusive /r/ after /ə/, as in *China and*, and after /ɪə/, as in *idea of*. In these environments, pronunciations without /r/ sound stilted or foreign. In other environments, as in *law and*, *pa and*, *drawing*, while intrusive /r/

does occur in the non-RP accents, particularly those spoken in the south-east of England, it is still somewhat conspicuous in RP. Intrusive /r/ in these environments is socially stigmatized to a certain extent—the /r/ is felt to be 'incorrect' because it does not correspond to an *r* in the spelling—and many RP speakers try to avoid it, quite frequently without being entirely successful. For example, many BBC newsreaders, when reading a phrase such as *law and order*, have to pause or insert a glottal stop before *and* in order not to pronounce an /r/.

Table 2.2 gives some indication of the occurrence of these different /r/s in different varieties of English:

2.2.   Australian, New Zealand and South African English

We now turn to an examination of the other 'English' types of English, and first the Southern Hemisphere varieties of Australia, New Zealand and South Africa. Strange as it may seem to those who speak these varieties, many people from other parts of the English-speaking world often have difficulty in telling one from the other—and indeed, as we have already suggested, there are many similarities between them in spite of the thousands of miles that separate the three countries.

The sociolinguistic situation (as far as English is concerned) is also similar in the three countries. There is, for example, very little regional variation in the English used, especially if compared to the amount of regional variation found in Britain—although there is probably rather more variation of this type in SAfEng than in the other two countries. (For the most part, regional variation in AusNZEng is lexical.) There is, on the other hand, a fair amount of social variation in all three types. This variation may be described as involving—as far as pronunciation is concerned— 'mild' and 'broad' accents. While all AusNZEng and SAfEng accents are phonologically very close to RP, phonetically there are differences: the 'mild' accents differ somewhat from RP, while the 'broad' accents differ considerably from RP. The 'mild' accents tend to be found towards the top of the social scale, particularly amongst older speakers. (RP is an accent which still has considerable prestige in these three countries, but there has been a very marked decline in this prestige in the last three decades or so.)

2.2.1.   AusEng

English has been spoken in Australia since 1788, and currently has about 15 million native speakers there.

2.2.1.1.   AusEng vowels: phonological differences from RP vowels

1.   Like south-of-England non-RP accents, AusEng has /iː/ rather than /ɪ/ in *very*, *many*, etc. Thus, *seedy* has the same vowel in both syllables in AusEng, while the vowels in *city* differ (see 2.1.2.(1)).
2.   Like south-of-England non-RP accents, but to a much greater extent, AusEng has /ə/ rather than /ɪ/ in unstressed syllables. Thus, not only does /ə/ occur in the final syllable of *horses* and *wanted*, it also occurs in the final syllable of *naked*, *David*, *honest*, *village*, etc. (see 2.1.2.(3)). This applies also in the unstressed syllables in words such as *begin* /bəgɪn/ and *laxity* /læksətiː/.
3.   AusEng follows RP in having /ɑː/ in *laugh*, *path*, *grass*, etc., but it differs from RP, and is more like non-RP north-of-England accents, in often having /æ/ in *dance*, *sample*, *plant*, *branch*, etc. (see 2.1.2.(4)). There is, however, a certain amount of regional variation. The individual word *castle* often has /æ/ in New South Wales and Queensland, while words from the *dance* set often have /ɑː/ in South Australia. There is also some social variation. Other things being equal, /ɑː/ forms are considered somewhat more prestigious than /æ/ forms.
4.   RP smoothing of /ɑuə/>/ɑː/, etc., does not occur (see 2.1.1.(2)).

2.2.1.2.   AusEng vowels: phonetic differences from RP vowels

Phonetic differences between RP and AusEng are considerable and, of course, most noticeable in 'broad' Australian accents. In some respects AusEng pronunciation resembles that of the London area of England more than RP, but there are many dissimilarities also. These phonetic differences are most obvious in the case of vowels, which are shown in Table 2.3. Although we are concentrating in this book on varieties empoyed by more educated speakers, it is possible in the case of AusNZEng and SAfEng accents to give more information by illustrating those varieties most unlike RP—i.e. 'broad' accents. 'Milder' accents are then those that are intermediate between 'broad' accents and RP.

   The distinctive differences are:

1.   AusEng front vowels tend to be closer than in RP (i.e. the body of the tongue is closer to the palate).
2.   Some of the diphthongs are wider than in RP (i.e. the difference between the open first element and close second element is greater in AusEng than in RP), but there is much social variation in the quality of the first element.
3.   There is a tendency for the diphthong to be 'slower', i.e. with

Table 2.3.   *Phonetic differences between broad AusEng and RP vowels*

		RP	Broad AusEng
bid	/ɪ/	[ɪ]	[i̯]
bed	/ɛ/	[ɛ]	[e̯]
bad	/æ/	[æ]	[ɛ̯]
pot	/ɒ/	[ɒ]	[ɔ̯]
putt	/ʌ/	[ɐ]	[ɐ˞]
put	/ʊ/	[ʊ]	[ʊ]
bee	/i:/	[ii]	[ɜ·ɪ]
bay	/ei/	[eɪ]	[a·ɪ]
buy	/ai/	[aɪ]	[ɒ·ɪ]~[ɒ·ə]
boy	/ɔi/	[ɔɪ]	[o·ɪ]
boot	/u:/	[uu]	[ʉʉ˞]
boat	/ou/	[ɵu]	[ɒ·ʉ]~[ɐ·ə]
bout	/au/	[aʊ]	[æ·ʉ]~[æ·ᴅ]~[ɛ·u̜]
peer	/ɪə/	[ɪə]	[i:]
pair	/ɛə/	[ɛə]	[e:]
paw	/ɔ:/	[ɔ:]	[o:]~[oɐ]
bard	/ɑ:/	[ɑ:]	[a:]
bird	/ɜ:/	[ɜ:]	[ə:]

a longer first element, than in RP, and even for diphthongs to become monophthongized, as in /ai/ as [ɒ·ɪ~ɒ·ˈ~ɒ·ᵊ].

4.   The /ɑ:/ vowel is a very front [a:] in comparison to most other varieties of English.

5.   Word-final /ə/ is often very open, e.g. *ever* [evɐ].

6.   The /ʊ/ vowel usually receives much more lip-rounding than in EngEng.

2.2.1.3.   AusEng consonants

For AusEng consonants, we can note the following:

1.   AusEng is non-rhotic and has linking and intrusive /r/ (see 2.1.3.(4)). AusEng /r/ is often more strongly retroflexed than in EngEng.

2.   Intervocalic /t/ as in *city*, *better*, may become the voiced flap—[d̺], as in NAmEng. However, this is by no means so common, standard, or consistent as it is in NAmEng, and [t] is also frequent in this environment. The glottal stop realization of /t/ may occur in *fit them*, as in RP, but not in any other environment. Glottal reinforcement as in *box*, *batch* does not occur (see 2.1.3.(3)).

3. AusEng often has an /l/ that is darker than in RP, e.g. *leaf* [ɫɜɪf].

2.2.1.4. Other AusEng pronunciation features

1. *Assume* etc. may be pronounced as /əšú:m/ rather than /əsú:m/~/əsjú:m/. Similarly, *presume* etc. can have /ž/ rather than /z/ or /zj/.
2. In some areas, /ɔ:/ may be heard in *off*, *often*, etc. more frequently than in RP.
3. *Australia*, *auction*, *salt*, which may have /ɒ/ or /ɔ:/ in RP, have only /ɒ/ in AusEng (see 2.1.1.(3)).
4. Days of the week tend to be pronounced with final /eɪ/ rather than RP /ɪ/, especially by younger speakers: *Monday* /mʌndeɪ/.
5. Initial /tj/, /dj/ may be pronounced as [č], [ǰ], e.g. *tune* [čə·ʉn], though this is not especially common in educated usage. (This feature is also found in many BritEng varieties.)
6. The sequence /lj/ often becomes /j/, as in *brilliant* (cf. 3.2.5.).
7. *Memo* is pronounced /mi:mou/, not /mɛmou/, as elsewhere.

2.2.1.5. Grammatical differences between AusEng and EngEng

At the level of educated speech and writing, there are very few obvious grammatical differences between AusEng and EngEng. It is, for example, usually not possible to tell if a text has been written by an English or Australian writer—unless by the vocabulary (see below). There are, however, a few distinctive tendencies:

1. The use of the auxiliaries *shall* and *should* with first-person subjects, as in *I shall go*, *We should like to see you*, is less usual in AusEng than in EngEng, and even in EngEng these are now increasingly replaced by *will* and *would*, as in *I will go/I'll go*, *We would like to see you*.
2. In EngEng, the following negative forms of *used to* are all possible:

He used not to go
He usedn't to go
He didn't use to go

with the first (older and more formal) construction being the most usual in writing. In AusEng, the third form is less usual than in EngEng, while the second form is probably more usual than in EngEng. Contracted forms without *to*—*He usedn't go*—are also more usual in AusEng than in EngEng.
3. For some speakers of EngEng, the auxiliary *do* is normally used in tag questions in sentences with the auxiliary *ought*: *He ought to go, didn't he?* In AusEng, *do* is not used in such cases;

instead, *should* or *ought* would occur (i.e. *shouldn't he?*, *oughtn't he?* in the above sentence).

4. The use of *have* in expressing possession, as in *I have a new car*, is more usual in EngEng than in AusEng, where *got*, as in *I've got a new car*, is preferred.

5. EngEng permits all the following double-object constructions (with some regional variation):

I'll give it him
I'll give him it
I'll give it to him

The construction with *to* is probably the most frequent in EngEng, especially in the south of England, and it is this form which is the most usual in AusEng (see also 4.1.1.4.).

6. In EngEng, it is quite usual for collective nouns to take plural verbs:

The government have made a mistake
The team are playing very badly

The reverse is the usual case in AusEng, where the above two sentences would tend to have the singular forms *has* and *is*, respectively (see also 4.1.2.2.).

7. In colloquial AusEng, the feminine pronoun *she* can be used to refer to inanimate nouns and in impersonal constructions:

She'll be right ('Everything will be all right')
She's a stinker today ('The weather is excessively hot today').

8. In some constructions AusEng may use an infinitive rather than a participle: *Some people delay to pay their tax* (cf. 4.1.1.4.).

9. USEng-style adverbial placement may occur: *He already has done it* (see 4.1.3.).

10. AusEng, like USEng, may have, for example, *Have you ever gone to London?* where EngEng would often prefer *Have you ever been to London?*

11. Some AusEng speakers use *whenever* to refer to a single occasion, as in NIrEng (see 5.2.2.).

12. The past participle forms *known, blown, sown, mown, grown, thrown, shown, flown* are often pronounced with final /ən/ rather than /n/, e.g. *known* /nouən/.

2.2.1.6. Lexical differences between EngEng and AusEng

Vocabulary differences between the Australasian varieties and EngEng are very small when compared to differences between the 'English' and 'American' varieties, hence the brevity of the word lists in this section. They are, however, numerous enough at the level of colloquial vocabulary. Some of the differences between EngEng and AusEng vocabulary are the result of borrowings into AusEng from Australian aboriginal languages. Well-known examples of such loans include *boomerang*, *dingo* (a wild dog) and *billabong* (a cut-off river channel), as well as many names for indigenous flora and fauna. In other cases the differences are purely intra-English. We give a short list of these below by way of illustration of types of lexical difference. Word lists consisting only of corresponding words in two dialects are often misleading, since differences can be quite subtle and may involve differences in frequency of use, style, or in only one particular sub-sense of a word. We therefore supplement the list with notes.

	AusEng	*EngEng*
1.	*to barrack for*	*to support*
2.	*bludger*	*a loafer, sponger*
3.	*footpath*	*pavement*
4.	*frock*	*dress*
5.	*get*	*fetch*
6.	*goodday*	*hello*
7.	*gumboots*	*wellington boots*
8.	*(one-storey) house*	*bungalow*
9.	*lolly*	*sweet*
10.	*paddock*	*field*
11.	*parka*	*anorak*
12.	*picture theatre*	*cinema*
13.	*radiator*	*(electric) fire*
14.	*sedan*	*saloon car*
15.	*singlet*	*vest*
16.	*station*	*stock farm*
17.	*station wagon*	*estate car*
18.	*stove*	*cooker*
19.	*stroller*	*push-chair*
20.	*wreckers*	*breakers*

Notes

1. *To barrack for* is a term used for support at, for example, football matches and of sports teams: *Who do you barrack for?* The term *to barrack* is known in EngEng but in the meaning of 'shouting abuse or unfavourable comments' at sports teams, and is now somewhat old-fashioned.
2. *Bludger* is colloquial only.
3. In EngEng, *footpath* refers to a path across fields, through woods, etc., while *pavement* refers to a pathway beside a road or

street. In AusEng, *footpath* covers both. Both *pavement* and *sidewalk* do occur, however, in certain areas of Australia.

4.   Both varieties permit both words. *Frock*, however, sounds old-fashioned in EngEng and is not used in advertising as it is in AusEng.

5.   *Get* is widely used in both varieties, but usages such as *I'll fetch it for you* are much less usual in AusEng than in EngEng.

6.   *Goodday* [gədei] is a common, colloquial form of greeting in AusEng.

7.   *Gumboots* is understood in EngEng but sounds rather archaic. Both varieties also use the term *rubber boots*.

8.   EngEng distinguishes between *bungalow* 'a one-storey house' and *house* 'a two or more storey house', although *house* is also a generic term covering both. In Australia (where, in fact, bungalows are a good deal more common than in Britain), this distinction is not made. *Bungalow*, however, is used in AusEng to refer to a less substantial construction such as a summer house, beach bungalow, etc.

9.   In EngEng, *lolly* is an abbreviation of *lollipop* (a word of Romany origin), which is a sweet on a stick, designed for licking. In AusEng, *lolly* is a generic term corresponding to EngEng *sweet*. *Sweet* is used in AusEng, but usually as a rather formal shop-type word.

10.   The word *paddock* is used in EngEng with the more restricted meaning of a field that is used for grazing horses. The AusEng usage refers to any piece of fenced-in land. *Field* is used in AusEng with abstract meaning and also in reference to, for example, a *football field* (=EngEng *football pitch*). Many words referring to European-type countryside features, such as *brook*, *stream*, *meadow*, are unusual or poetic in AusEng.

11.   The word *parka* is known in EngEng but in recent years has been replaced by *anorak*, although some manufacturers may make a distinction, using these terms, between different types of coat. Both words are loans from Eskimo.

12.   *Cinema* is in fact used in both varieties, but is rather higher style in AusEng. One doesn't say *picture theatre* in EngEng, but both varieties have the informal phrase *going to the pictures*.

13.   *Radiator* is used in EngEng, but only with reference to hot water or oil radiators, e.g. those used in central-heating systems. In EngEng both portable and fixed heaters consisting of electrically heated bars are known as *fires*.

14.   Here AusEng follows NAmEng.

15.   The garment referred to here is an undershirt. *Singlet* is known and used in EngEng, but *vest* is not usual in AusEng.

16.   In AusEng a *station* refers to a large cattle or sheep farm

(besides having the meaning common to all forms of English, as in *railway station*).
17.   Here AusEng follows NAmEng.
18.   *Cooker* is not usual in AusEng, while both *cooker* and *stove* are used in EngEng.
19.   *Stroller* is known in EngEng, but is not so widely used as *push-chair*. Some forms of AusEng also use *push-chair* or *'pushy'*.
20.   The reference here is to premises dealing with old, broken down, or crashed cars.

Most lexical differences within the English-speaking world can be found at the level of colloquial speech, and especially in that faddish, often transitory form known as 'slang'. AusEng slang or colloquial expressions not known in EngEng include:

to chunder	'to vomit'
crook	'ill, angry'
a dag	'an eccentric person'
a drongo	'a fool'
to rubbish	'to pour scorn on'
a sheila	'a girl'
to front up	'to arrive, present oneself somewhere'
to bot	'to cadge, borrow'
hard yakka	'hard work'
to shoot through	'to leave'
tucker	'food'
a wog	'a germ'
a spell	'a rest, break'
a park	'a parking space'
to shout	'to buy something' (e.g. a round of drinks) 'for someone'
a humpy	'a shelter, hut'
to chyack	'to tease'
an offsider	'a partner, companion'
a chook	'a chicken'
a larrikin	'a young ruffian'
to dob	'to plonk' (something down on something)
to fine up	'to improve' (of weather)
beaut	'very nice, great'
uni	'university' (cf. NZEng varsity)
to retrench	'to sack, make redundant'
financial	'paid up' (as of a member of a club)
interstate	'in another' (Australian) state

For a note on AusEng spelling, see 4.2.1.(1).

2.2.1.7. Usage

1. It is usual in AusEng to use *thanks* rather than *please* in requests: *Can I have a cup of tea, thanks?*
2. Colloquial abbreviations are more frequent than in EngEng: e.g. *beaut* 'beautiful, beauty'; *uni* 'university'.
3. Abbreviated nouns ending in -/i:/ are more common in colloquial AusEng than in EngEng, and many forms occur which are known in EngEng: e.g. *truckie* 'truck driver'; *tinnie* 'tin'—used especially of a can of beer.
4. Abbreviated nouns ending in -/ou/ are much more common in colloquial AusEng than in EngEng, and many forms occur which are unknown in EngEng: e.g. *arvo* 'afternoon'; *muso* 'musician'.
5. Abbreviated personal names ending in -/zə/ are common, e.g. *Bazza* 'Barry'; *Mezza* 'Mary'.

2.2.2. NZEng

English has been spoken in New Zealand since the early 19th century and has about 3 million native speakers there.

2.2.2.1. New Zealand vowels

Phonetically and phonologically, NZEng accents are very similar to AusEng, and 'mild' AusEng and NZEng accents are difficult for outsiders to tell apart, particularly in the case of older speakers. NZEng is like AusEng in having /i:/ in *very* etc., and /ə/ in *naked* etc. It also has wider and slower diphthongs than RP, a very front /ɑ:/, and lacks smoothing (see 2.1.1.). The phonetic differences between RP and NZEng vowels are indicated in Table 2.4. The major characteristics of the NZEng vowel system are the following:

1. Phonetically speaking, the NZEng vowel /ɪ/ as in *bid* is a central vowel in the region of [ə]. The contrast between AusEng *bid* [bid] and NZEng [bəd] is very clear, and the most noticeable indication of whether a speaker is an Australian or a New Zealander. As a further, linked development, the vowel /ɪ/ = [ə] has become merged with /ʊ/ after /w/, so that, for example, *women* has become identical in pronunciation to *woman* (see also (7) below). Phonologically, we can say that younger New Zealanders, at least, have no distinction between /ɪ/ and /ə/, and thus pronounce, for example, *finish* [fənəš], *Philip* [fələp], as compared to AusEng [filəp] and RP [fɪlɪp]. This means that there is no need to postulate /ə/ as a separate vowel in more recent varieties of NZEng—we recognize only the vowel /ɪ/, pronounced [ə].

2. In one phonological context, the RP vowel /ə/ corresponds not to /ɪ/, as discussed in (1) above, but to /ʌ/. In unstressed word-final position, NZEng has a vowel identical to the stressed vowel of *putt*, e.g. *butter* /bʌtʌ/. Notice that this applies to the indefinite article *a*: *a cup* /ʌ kʌp/.

3. The front vowels /ɛ/ as in *bed* and /æ/ as in *bad* are even closer than in AusEng: *bed* [bẹd], *bad* [bɛ̣d].

4. For most speakers, as in South Australia, most words in the set of *dance, sample, grant, branch* have /ɑ:/ = [a:] rather than /æ/. A few words in the *laugh* set, however, generally have /æ/. This is especially true of *telegraph, graph*.

5. There is a strong and growing tendency for /ɪə/ and /ɛə/ to merge, so that pairs such as *beer, bear* are pronounced identically: [bẹ: ~ bẹə].

6. For many speakers, /ɒ/ and /ou/ are merged before /l/, so that *doll* and *dole* are identical. Distinctions between other vowels may also be neutralized before /l/, as well as before /r/, so that *pull* and *pool, fellow* and *fallow, will* and *wool*, and *Derry, dairy* and *dearie* may be identical. Like in AusEng, /l/ is dark in all positions, and there is also an increasing tendency to lip-rounding and vocalization of /l/, i.e. syllable-final /l/ is either [ɫ̩] or a vowel with a quality around [o], e.g. *bell* [bẹɫ̩ ~ beo].

7. Unlike AusEng, the vowel /ʊ/ tends to be unrounded, as in many types of EngEng (see 2.1.1.).

8. The /ɜ:/ vowel of *bird* has a considerable degree of lip-rounding, as in WEng (see 2.3.1.).

2.2.2.2. NZEng consonants

1. In NZEng, the /ʍ/ of *which* has been strongly maintained much more so even than in RP. However, it is now being lost in the speech of younger New Zealanders.

2. Intervocalic /t/ as in *city, better* is variably a voiced flap, as in AusEng.

3. Most forms of NZEng are non-rhotic (see 2.1.3.), with linking and intrusive /r/, but the local accents of the southern area of the South Island, comprising parts of Otago and Southland, are rhotic. The area concerned centres on Invercargill and includes Gore, Tapanui, Winton, Nightcaps and Ohai (see Map 2). This phenomenon is known to New Zealanders as the 'Southland burr' and is often ascribed to the influence of settlers from Scotland and Ireland.

4. The word *with* is pronounced /wɪθ/, as in ScotEng, CanEng and some forms of USEng, rather than /wɪð/, as in EngEng.

Table 2.4.   *Phonetic differences between NZEng and RP vowels*

		RP	NZEng
bid	/ɪ/	[ɪ]	[ə]
bed	/ɛ/	[ɛ]	[e̞]
bad	/æ/	[æ]	[ɛ̞]
pot	/ɒ/	[ɒ]	[ɒ]
putt	/ʌ/	[ɐ]	[ɐ˧]
put	/ʊ/	[ʊ]	[ɤ]
bee	/iː/	[ii]	[ɜ·ɪ]
bay	/ei/	[eɪ]	[a·ɪ]
buy	/ai/	[aɪ]	[ɑ·ɪ]
boy	/ɔi/	[ɔɪ]	[o·ɪ]
boot	/uː/	[uu]	[ə·ʉ]
boat	/ou/	[ɵu]	[ɐ·ʉ ~ ɐ·ɵ]
bout	/ɑu/	[ɑu]	[æ·ʉ]
peer	/ɪə/	[ɪə]	[eə]
pair	/ɛə/	[ɛə]	[eə]
paw	/ɔː/	[ɔː]	[o̞ː]
bard	/ɑː/	[ɑː]	[aː]
bird	/ɜː/	[ɜː]	[ø̞ː]

2.2.2.3.   NZEng grammar

1. NZEng resembles AusEng in avoiding *shall*, *should*; in lacking totally the construction *I'll give it him*; and, in the written language at least, in preferring singular verb agreement as in *The team is playing badly*.

2.   Many NZEng speakers also take *shall*-avoidance one stage further than AusEng speakers, in the ScotEng manner (see 5.1.4.), and use constructions such as *Will I close the window?* rather than EngEng *Shall I close the window?*, NAmEng *Should I close the window?*

3.   Corresponding to EngEng *at the weekend* and NAmEng *on the weekend* many NZEng speakers have *in the weekend*.

2.2.2.4.   NZEng lexis

In most respects, NZEng agrees with either AusEng (e.g. *lolly* and many of the other items in 2.2.1.6.) or with EngEng. NZEng usages include:

NZEng	*EngEng*
tramping	'hiking'
to farewell	'to say goodbye to'
to front	'to turn up, appear'
to uplift	'to pick up, collect'

a domain	'a recreation area'
to jack up	'to arrange'
an identity	'a character'

Other more colloquial usages include:

a joker	'a guy, bloke'
to skite	'to boast'
to wag	'to play truant'
a hoon	'a yob'
a bach (from bachelor)	'a cabin, cottage'
a crib	'a cabin, cottage' (southern South Island only)
a Kiwi	'a New Zealander'
lairy	'loud' (of colours—in some areas only)

2.2.2.5. Maori lexis

The indigenous population of New Zealand are the Maori, whose arrival in New Zealand antedates that of Europeans by several hundred and perhaps as much as a thousand years. There are today about 300 000 Maori in New Zealand—about 10 per cent of the population—and about 100 000 of these are native speakers of Maori, which is a Polynesian language related to Tongan, Samoan, Tahitian, Hawaiian and many others. All Maori speakers, however, can also speak English. Many New Zealand place-names are of Maori origin, e.g. Whangarei, Te Anau. A rather large number of Maori words have found their way into the usage of English speakers in New Zealand, most of them, however, being used solely in connection with Maori culture. The following words—the list is not exhaustive—can be found in New Zealand books and newspapers, without translation into English, indicating that most New Zealanders know what they mean:

Maori/NZEng	*EngEng*
aroha	'love'
haka	'posture dance'
hui	'assembly'
iwi	'tribe'
kaumatua	'elder'
kaupapa	'plan, rule'
mana	'power, honour'
marae	'meeting ground'
pa	'village'
paepae	'threshold'

pakeha	'white person, New Zealander of European origin'
powhiri	'welcome'
rangatira	'chief'
rangatiratanga	'kingdom'
runanga	'assembly, debate'
tangata	'people'
taniwha	'monster'
tapu	'sacred'
taua	'war'
tauiwi	'foreigner'
umu	'oven'
waka	'canoe'
whare	'house'
whakapapa	'genealogy'
whenua	'land, country'

Of these, the word *mana* is also used in non-Maori contexts. The word *tapu* is essentially the same as the English word *taboo*, which was borrowed into English from Tongan. *Pakeha* and *Maori* are the terms normally used to refer to the two major ethnic groups in the country.

2.2.2.6.   Usage

1.   As in AusEng, certain abbreviated forms not found in EngEng or NAmEng are common in colloquial speech, e.g. *beaut* 'beautiful, beauty'; *ute* 'utility vehicle, pick-up truck'; *varsity* 'university'.
2.   As in AusEng, *thanks* can be used where other varieties of English normally have *please*: *Can I have a cup of tea, thanks?*
3.   As in AusEng, although the words involved are not in all cases the same, colloquial abbreviations ending in -/ou/ are common: *arvo* 'afternoon'; *smoko* 'break, rest period'.
4.   As in AusEng, although the words involved are not in all cases the same, colloquial abbreviations ending in -/i:/ are common: *boatie* 'boating enthusiast'; *postie* 'postman, delivery worker' (also found in ScotEng).

2.2.3.   SAfEng

The population of the Republic of South Africa is about 30 million. The African majority, about 70 per cent of the population, speak Bantu languages such as Zulu, Xhosa, Sotho and Tswana. About 20 per cent of the population speak Afrikaans, a language of

Map No. 2. New Zealand South Island

European origin related to Dutch; and a small percentage speak languages of Indian origin such as Hindi and Tamil. The surviving indigenous languages of the area, the Khoisan (Bushman and 'Hottentot') languages, are in a stronger position in neighbouring Namibia and Botswana than they are in South Africa itself.

English has had significant numbers of speakers in South Africa since the 1820s and is currently spoken natively by about 2 million whites and nearly 1 million 'coloured' (mixed race) and Indian-origin speakers. English is also very widely spoken as a second language. Forms of English which closely resemble SAfEng are also spoken natively in Zimbabwe, as well as by relatively small groups of whites in Namibia, Zambia and Kenya.

In what follows we confine our attention to the English of native speakers in South Africa.

2.2.3.1.   SAfEng vowels

Just as with AusNZEng, there is a certain amount of variation in the pronunciation of SAfEng, ranging from RP or near-RP to 'broad' SAfEng. SAfEng is characterized by the following vocalic phenomena:

1.   Like RP and NZEng, SAfEng has /ɑ:/ in the *dance* set of words. This distinguishes it from most forms of AusEng.
2.   The feature which most readily distinguishes between SAfEng and AusNZEng is the very back pronunciation of /ɑ:/ = [ɑ:] in *car*, *dance*, etc., contrasting with AusNZEng front [a:].
3.   The SAfEng pronunciation of /ɪ/ is also distinctive in that it has both the high front [i] of AusEng and the centralized [ə] of NZEng. In SAfEng, however, these two pronunciations constitute allophonic variants: [i] occurs before and after the velar consonants /k/, /g/ and /ŋ/, before /š/, after /h/, and word-initially; [ə] occurs elsewhere. Thus *big* is [big], but *bit* is [bət].
4.   There is an even stronger tendency in SAfEng than in AusEng for diphthongs to be monophthongized (see Table 2.5).
5.   SAfEng shares with AusNZEng the occurrence of /ə/ in the unstressed syllables of *naked*, *village*, etc.
6.   SAfEng also agrees with AusNZEng in having /i:/ in the final syllable of *very*, *many*, etc.

Table 2.5.   SAfEng vowels

		RP	SAfEng
bid	/ɪ/	[ɪ]	[ə]
bed	/ɛ/	[ɛ]	[e]
bad	/æ/	[æ]	[ɛ]
pot	/ɒ/	[ɒ]	[ɔ]
putt	/ʌ/	[ɐ]	[ɐ˧]
put	/ʊ/	[ʊ]	[u]
bee	/i:/	[ii̯]	[i:]
bay	/ei/	[eɪ]	[ɐe]
buy	/ai/	[aɪ]	[ɑ·ᵊ]
boy	/ɔi/	[ɔɪ]	[oe]
boot	/u:/	[uu̯]	[ʉ:]
boat	/ou/	[ɵʊ]	[ʌ˧·ᵊ]
bout	/ɑu/	[ɑʊ]	[æ·ᵊ]
peer	/ɪə/	[ɪə]	[e:]
pair	/ɛə/	[ɛə]	[e:]
paw	/ɔ:/	[ɔ:]	[o:]
bard	/ɑ:/	[ɑ:]	[ɑ:]
bird	/ɜ:/	[ɜ:]	[ø˧:]

2.2.3.2. SAfEng consonants

1. There is a tendency, possibly as a result of Afrikaans influence, for /p/, /t/, /č/, /k/ to be unaspirated: *pin* RP [pʰɪn], SAfEng [pən].
2. As in AusNZEng, there is a tendency for intervocalic /t/, as in *better*, to be a voiced flap [d̪], although this is not so widespread or consistent as in NAmEng.
3. In a number of varieties of SAfEng, the 'dark *l*' [ɫ] allophone of /l/ as in *hill* does not occur (see 2.1.3.(1)).
4. SAfEng is *r*-less, lacking non-prevocalic *r* (except in Afrikaans-influenced English varieties). Very many varieties of SAfEng also lack both intrusive *r* and linking *r* (see 2.1.3.(4)): thus, *four o'clock* [fo:(ʔ)əklɔk], *law and order* [lo:n̩o:də]. SAfEng is alone among the 'English' varieties of English in having this characteristic.

There is a strong tendency for /r/ to be a flap [ɾ], unlike the frictionless continuant [ɹ] of RP or AusNZEng. (Afrikaans speakers often use a trilled [r].)

5. /tj/, /dj/ often are realized as [č], [ǰ], as in many EngEng varieties: *tune* [čʉ:n] (cf. AusEng).

2.2.3.3. SAfEng grammar and usage

There appear to be even fewer grammatical differences between SAfEng and EngEng than between AusNZEng and EngEng, especially at the level of educated speech.

1. A common 'broad' SAfEng feature is the use of the all-purpose response question *is it?*, invariable for person, tense or auxiliary, which corresponds to the complex series *do they, can't he, shouldn't we, will you*, etc. used in other varieties:

He's gone to town.—Oh, is it? (=EngEng *Oh, has he?*)

2. In 'broader' varieties of SAfEng it is possible in certain constructions and contexts to delete object noun phrases (NPs) after verbs which must have NPs in other varieties, e.g.:

Have you got?
Have you sent?
Did you put?

3. Complement structures of *adjective + infinitive* occur where other varieties have *adjective + of + participle*:

This plastic is capable to withstand heat (=This plastic is capable of withstanding heat)

4.   Non-negative *no* occurs as an introductory particle:

How are you?
No, I'm fine, thanks

The force of this is often to negate assumptions made in the preceding question or comment.

2.2.3.4.   SAfEng lexis

As with AusNZEng, the contact of SAfEng with other languages has had an effect on its vocabulary. Among the better known borrowings are:

from Zulu:
impi   'African warrior band'
indaba   'conference'

from Afrikaans:
dorp   'village'
kraal   'African village'
sjambok   'whip'
veld   'flat, open country'

Differences within formal English vocabulary are not especially numerous but include:

SAfEng	*EngEng*
bioscope	cinema
location	(Black) *ghetto*
reference book	*identity document*
robot	*traffic light*

2.3.   Welsh English

English is the native language of about 80 per cent of the population of Wales, i.e. about 2.25 million people. Many of these have some competence in Welsh. The remaining 20 per cent, about 0.5 million or so, are native speakers of Welsh and are all bilingual in English.

Until quite recently, in most areas of Wales, English was a second language learnt in school (as was the case in the Highlands of Scotland). Although this is no longer true and a majority of people in Wales are now native speakers of English, the effect is that Welsh English, at the level of educated speech and writing, is not much different from that of England, except phonetically and phonologically. There are, of course, distinctly Welsh lexical items and grammatical constructions, often due to the influence of Welsh, but Welsh Standard English cannot be said to be particularly different from EngEng. Most differences are found at the level of more localized dialects (see Wells, 1982 and Hughes and Trudgill, 1987).

2.3.1. WEng vowels

The Welsh English vowel system is, with some regional variation, as in Table 2.6 and on the recording.

Table 2.6. WEng vowels

/ɪ/	[ɪ]	*bid*
/ɛ/	[ɛ]	*bed*
/æ/	[a]	*bad, pass, above, sofa*
/ɒ/	[ɔ]	*pot, object* (v.)
/ʌ/	[ə]	*putt, famous, rubber*
/ʊ/	[ʊ]	*put*
/iː/	[iː]	*bee*
/ei/	[eː]	*bake*
/ai/	[əɪ]	*buy*
/ɔi/	[ɔɪ]	*boy*
/uː/	[uː]	*boot*
/ou/	[oː]	*boat, board*
/ɑu/	[əʊ]	*bout*
/ɛə/	[ɛː]	*pair*
/ɔː/	[ɔː]	*sort, paw*
/ɑː/	[aː]	*bard, calm*
/ɜː/	[øː]	*bird*
/ɛi/	[eɪ]	*bait*
/ɔu/	[o̞ʊ]	*blow*

The principal phonological differences between WEng and RP are the following:

1. *last, dance*, etc. tend to have /æ/ rather than /ɑː/ for most WEng speakers, although /ɑː/ is found for many speakers in some words.
2. Unstressed orthographic *a* tends to be /æ/ rather than /ə/, e.g. *sofa* [soːfa].
3. Unstressed orthographic *o* tends to be /ɒ/ rather than /ə/, e.g. *condemn* /kɒndɛm/.
4. There is no contrast between /ʌ/ and /ə/: *rubber* /rəbə/.
5. There is, in many varieties, an additional contrast, between /ei/ and /ɛi/:

made	/meid/	[meːd]
maid	/mɛid/	[me̞ɪd]

Words with /ɛi/ are typically those spelt with *ai* or *ay*.
6.   There is, in many varieties, an additional contrast between
/ou/ and /ɔu/:

| *nose* | /nouz/ | [noːz] |
| *knows* | /nɔuz/ | [no̝ʊz] |

7.   Many words which have /ɔ:/ in RP have the vowel /ou/ = [oː]
in many WEng varieties. Thus:

	RP	*WEng*
so	[søu]	[soː]
soar	[sɔ:]	[soː]

Note, however, that *port*, *paw* still have /ɔ:/ in WEng.
8.   The vowels /ɪə/, /ʊə/ do not occur in many varieties of WEng.
Fear is /fiːjə/, *poor* is /puːwə/. Similarly, *fire* is /faijə/.
9.   Words such as *tune*, *music* have /tiʊn/, /mɪʊzɪk/ rather than
/tjuːn/, /mjuːzɪk/.

2.3.2.   WEng consonants

1.   Educated WEng is not rhotic with a few exceptions in the east
and far south-west of the country; intrusive and linking /r/ do
occur; and /r/ is often a flapped [ɾ].
2.   Voiceless plosives tend to be strongly aspirated, and in
word-final position are generally released and without glottalization, e.g. *pit* [pʰɪtʰ].
3.   /l/ is clear [l] in all positions.
4.   There is a strong tendency for intervocalic consonants to be
lengthened before unstressed syllables:

| *butter* | [bətʰːə] |
| *money* | [mənːi] |

5.   The Welsh consonants /ɬ/ and /x/ occur in place-names and
loan-words from Welsh. /ɬ/ is a voiceless, lateral fricative, and /x/ is
a voiceless velar fricative as in Scots *loch* or German *acht*, e.g.:

| *Llanberis* | /ɬanbérɪs/ |
| *bach* | /baːx/ (term of endearment) |

2.3.3   Non-systemic pronunciation differences

1.   For some WEng speakers, /g/ is absent in the following two
words:

	WEng	*RP*
language	/læŋwɛǰ/	/læŋgwɪǰ/
longer	/lɒŋə/	/lɒŋgə/

2. For some WEng speakers, /ʊ/ occurs in both of the following words:

	WEng	*RP*
comb	/kʊm/	/koum/
tooth	/tʊθ/	/tu:θ/

2.3.4. WEng grammar

The following features can be observed in the speech of even some educated WEng speakers but are not usually encountered in written Welsh English:

1. The use of the universal tag question *isn't it?*, invariable for main clause person, tense or auxiliary:

You're going now, isn't it? (=EngEng *aren't you?*)
They do a lot of work, isn't it? (=EngEng *don't they?*)

2. The use of *will* for *will be*:

Is he ready? No, but he will in a minute.

3. The use of predicate object inversion for emphasis:

WEng: *Coming home tomorrow he is*
EngEng: *He's coming home tomorrow/It's tomorrow he's coming home*

4. The use of negative *too*:

WEng: *I can't do that, too*
EngEng: *I can't do that, either*

5. The use of adjective and adverb reduplication for emphasis:

WEng: *It was high, high*
EngEng: *It was very high*

2.3.5. WEng lexis

Surprisingly few Welsh loan-words are used in standard WEng. Common words include:

del	/dɛl/	a term of endearment
eisteddfod	/aistɛ́ðvɒd/	a competitive arts festival (This word is known to EngEng speakers, who generally pronounce it /aistɛ́ðfəd/.)
llymru	/ɬəmri:/	porridge dish

Different WEng usages of English words found in some parts of Wales include:

delight	'interest'	(e.g. *a delight in languages*)
rise	'get, buy'	(e.g. *I'll rise the drinks*)
tidy	'good, nice'	(e.g. *a tidy car*)

Again, most vocabulary differences are at the level of non-standard or colloquial usage.

3
The pronunciation of North American English

The sociolinguistic situation in the United States and Canada, as far as pronunciation is concerned, is rather different from that of the rest of the English-speaking world. There is more regional variation in NAmEng pronunciation than in AusNZEng and SAfEng, yet there is no universally accepted totally regionless standard pronunciation as in EngEng.

In this chapter we will begin by giving an outline of one USEng accent—an accent employed by some educated white middle-class speakers from the central east-coast region. We will then point to differences between this accent and RP. Next we will discuss regional differences within NAmEng pronunciation, concentrating on varieties of educated speech and omitting mention of most lower-prestige accents.

3.1. North American English vowels

Table 3.1 and the first US speaker on the recording illustrate the vowel system of the USEng accent described above. Note that, to aid comparison, vowel symbols have been chosen which are closest to those used in Chapter 2 for the 'English' type accents rather than those typically used by American writers. Note also that this phonological analysis is not so widely accepted as the analysis of RP vowels given in 2.1.1. In particular, the identification of vowel phonemes before /r/ (especially the vowels of *bird*, *port* and *furry*) is not entirely uncontroversial in view of the considerable allophonic variation before /r/ : /i/—*peer* [pɪəɹ]; /ei/—*pair* [pɛəɹ]; /ai/—*fire* [faɪəɹ]; /u/—*tour* [tʊəɹ]; /au/—*tower* [taʊəɹ]; /ɔ/—*port* [pɔəɹt]; /ə/—*bird* [bəːɹd] ~ [bɹ̩d]. This allophonic variation is particularly clear on the recording, suggesting especially that *port*, *boring*,

Table 3.1.   *USEng vowel system (Central East Coast)**

/ɪ/	*bid, mirror, wanted*
/ɛ/	*bed, merry*
/æ/	*bad, marry, path, dance, half, banana*
/ɑ/	*pot, bard, father, calm, horrid*
/ʌ/	*putt, hurry*
/ʊ/	*put*
/i/	*bee, very, peer*
/ei/	*bay, pair, Mary*
/ai/	*buy, fire, night, ride*
/ɔi/	*boy*
/u/	*boot, tour*
/ou/	*boat*
/ɑu/	*bout, loud, tower*
/ɔ/	*paw, port, talk, boring, long, pore*
/ə/	*about, sofa, bird, furry, butter*

*The words in Table 3.1. are also used in the recording for USEng (Mid-Western) and CanEng (see page 145).

pore, etc., might be better analysed as having /our/ rather than /ɔr/.

3.1.1.   NAmEng vowels: phonological differences from RP

1.   NAmEng agrees with all other English varieties we have discussed in differing from RP by having /i/ rather than /ɪ/ in *very* etc. (However, a number of south-eastern and eastern USA varieties *do* have /ɪ/ here.)

2.   The three RP vowels /ɒ/, /æ/ and /ɑ:/ correspond to only two vowels in NAmEng—/ɑ/ and /æ/. This, combined with the phonetic difference between RP /ɒ/ and USEng /ɑ/ and a difference in vowel distribution in many sets of words, makes for a complicated set of correspondences. When this is further combined with a different distribution in word sets of the vowels /ɑ/ and /ɔ/ (NAm): /ɒ/ and /ɔ:/ (RP) and the rhotic/non-rhotic difference, the picture becomes even more complex:

	RP	*USEng*
bad	æ	æ
Datsun	æ	ɑ
Bogota	ɒ	ou
pot	ɒ	ɑ
cough	ɒ	ɔ
long	ɒ	ɔ

paw	ɔː	ɔ
port	ɔː	ɔr
bard	ɑː	ɑr
path	ɑː	æ
dance	ɑː	æ
half	ɑː	æ
ban*a*na	ɑː	æ
father	ɑː	ɑ

This chart illustrates the following points:

(a) In very many words spelled with *a*, the correspondence is straightforward: in *cat*, *bad*, *man*, etc., RP /æ/ = NAmEng /æ/. Similarly, in very many words spelled with *o*, the correspondence is also reliable: in *pot*, *top*, *nod*, etc., RP /ɒ/ = NAmEng /ɑ/.

The remaining points are somewhat problematic:

(b) Perhaps because in many varieties of USEng /æ/ tends to be rather closer than in RP (see below), many words felt to be 'foreign' have /ɑ/ in USEng corresponding to the /æ/ in RP. Thus *Milan* is /mɪlǽn/ in RP but may be /mɪlɑ́n/ in NAmEng, and *Datsun* in USEng is /dɑ́tsn/, as if it were spelled *Dotsun*. This tendency is not entirely uncomplicated, however, as there are some words, e.g. *khaki*, where the reverse correspondence is found, i.e. USEng /kǽki/, RP /kɑːkɪ/. (CanEng often has /kɑrki/.)

(c) Probably as a consequence of the fact that NAmEng /ɑ/ in *pot* is an unrounded vowel, 'foreign' words spelled with *o* tend to have /ou/ in NAmEng corresponding to /ɒ/ in EngEng:

	EngEng	*NAmEng*
Bogota	/bɒgətɑː/	/bougətɑ/
Carlos	/kɑːlɒs/	/kɑrlous/

(d) NAmEng does not have the RP distinction /ɒ/—/ɑː/ *bomb—balm*, and therefore has /ɑ/ not only in the set *pot, top*, but also for many words that have /ɑː/ in RP including *father*, *calm* (for many speakers), *rather* (for some speakers). Thus *father* rhymes with *bother*, and *bomb* with *balm* are pronounced the same.

(e) While both RP and the variety of NAmEng described here have a different vowel in *cot* than in *caught*—RP /kɒt/, /kɔːt/: NAmEng /kɑt/, /kɔt/—the distribution of words over these vowels differs somewhat. In some cases RP /ɒ/ corresponds to NAm /ɑ/, and RP /ɔː/ to NAm /ɔ/. But it is also the case that RP /ɒ/ corresponds to NAm /ɔ/ in words having an *o* before *ng*

Table 3.2.   Word distribution of /ɒ/—/ɑ/ and /ɔ:/—/ɔ/

RP /ɒ/	NAmEng /ɑ/	RP /ɔ:/	NAmEng /ɔ/
cot	*cot*		
top	*top*		
pot	*pot*		
pond	*pond*		
	calm		
	father		
	Milan		
		caught	*caught*
		taught	*taught*
		launch	*launch*
		bought	*bought*
		all	*all*
		tall	*tall*
		saw	*saw*
loss			*loss*
cross			*cross*
soft			*soft*
cough			*cough*
off			*off*
cloth			*cloth*
song			*song*
long			*long*
wrong			*wrong*

or one of the voiceless fricatives /f/, /θ/, /s/ (cf. 2.1.1.(3)). In some areas this also applies to *o* before *g* as in *dog, fog*. This is illustrated in Table 3.2. Foreign learners may find the distribution of /ɑ/ and /ɔ/ in USEng confusing and hard to learn. They can take comfort, however, from the fact that many NAmEng accents in fact do not distinguish between these two vowels at all (see 3.3. below).

(f) While RP does not distinguish between *gnaw* and *nor*, NAmEng being rhotic, does. (See *paw, port*, on chart.)

(g) Being rhotic, NAmEng has /r/ in *bard* etc. Note that the lack of the RP /ɒ/—/ɑ:/ distinction means that *cod* /kad/ and *card* /kard/ are distinguished only by means of the /r/ (cf. RP *cod* /kɒd/, *card* /kɑ:d/), while *starry* and *sorry* are perfect rhymes: USEng /stɑri/—/sɑri/, EngEng /stɑ:rɪ/—/sɒrɪ/.

(h) In words such as *path, laugh, grass*, where RP has /ɑ:/ before /θ/, /f/, /s/, NAmEng has /æ/.

(i) This applies also to RP /ɑ:/ before /nt/, /ns/, /nč/, /nd/, /mp/. Thus NAmEng agrees with northern English accents and many types of AusEng in having /æ/ rather than /ɑ:/ in *plant, dance, branch, sample*, etc.

(j) NAmEng, in this case unlike northern English accents, also has /æ/ in *half, banana, can't*.

3. The rhoticity of NAmEng has the consequence that the following RP vowels (derived historically from vowel + /r/) do not occur in NAmEng:

/ɪə/ in *dear* (=NAm /ir/)
/ɛə/ in *dare* (=NAm /eɪr/)
/ʊə/ in *tour* (=NAm /ur/)
/ɜ:/ in *bird* (=NAm /ər/—but see 3.1. above)

The final syllable in *idea*—identical in RP to the /ɪə/ of *peer, dear*—is best regarded as being /i/ + /ə/ in NAmEng.

3.1.2. NAmEng vowels: phonetic differences from RP

Perhaps all vowels in NAmEng are somewhat different from RP vowels. The major differences, however, are:

1. The vowel of *pot* is unrounded [ɑ] in NAmEng, rounded [ɒ] in RP.
2. The vowel /ɔ/ of *paw* in USEng tends to be shorter, more open and less rounded than the equivalent vowel /ɔ:/ in RP.
3. Very front realizations of /ou/ such as RP [øʉ] are not found in most varieties of NAmEng, a typical NAmEng pronunciation being [oʊ] (but see 3.3.1.1.(4) below).
4. The diphthong /ei/ may be closer in NAmEng, [eɪ] as opposed to RP [e̞ɪ].
5. The first element of /au/ tends to be more front in NAmEng than in RP: NAmEng [aʊ], RP [ɑʊ].

3.2. North American English consonants

1. Glottal reinforcement as found in RP (see 2.1.3.(3b)) is not found in NAmEng. Neither is [ʔ] found as an allophone of /t/ in most NAmEng varieties, except before /n/ *button* [bəʔn̩] or, in New York City and Boston, before /l/: *bottle* [bɑʔl̩]. Final /t/, however, is often unreleased in NAmEng, especially before a following consonant, as in *that man*.
2. The RP allophonic differentiation of /l/: [l] vs. [ɫ] (see 2.1.3.(1)) is either not found or not so strong in NAmEng. In most varieties, /l/ is fairly dark in all positions.
3. Intervocalic /t/, as in *better*, in NAmEng is most normally a

vocalic flap [ḍ], not unlike the flapped /r/, [ɾ], of ScotEng. In many varieties the result is a neutralization of the distribution between /t/ and /d/ in this position, i.e. *ladder* and *latter* both have [ḍ]. While the intervocalic consonants are identical, in some varieties the original distinction is preserved through vowel length, with the vowel before /d/ being longer: *ladder* [læ·dɹ], *latter* [læḍɹ]. In other varieties the distinction may be marginally preserved as /d/ = [d], /t/ = [ḍ].

This flapped [ḍ] is consistently used in NAmEng in *latter*, *city*, etc. by most speakers, except in very formal styles, where [t] may occur. In the suffix *-ity*, [ḍ] may vary with [t], as in *obscurity*, *electricity*. In *plenty*, *twenty*, etc. [nt] alternates with [n ~ n̥ ~ nd]. Thus *winner* and *winter* may or may not be identical.

4.   As we have noted, NAmEng is rhotic and has /r/ in *bird*, *card*, *car*, etc. (and in the word *colonel* [kɹnɬ]). Phonetically speaking, too, the /r/ is pronounced rather differently from that of RP. Acoustically the impression is one of greater retroflexion (the tip of the tongue is curled back further) than in RP, but in fact many Americans achieve this effect by the humping up of the body of the tongue rather than by actual retroflexion.

5.   As in AusEng, many USEng speakers have a strong tendency to reduce /lj/ to /j/ as in *million* /mɪjən/.

3.3.   Regional variation in United States English

Our examination of an educated central-eastern variety of USEng (3.1., 3.2.) has established the major differences between NAmEng phonology and that of the EngEng types. We now turn to an examination of some of the major regional variants of educated NAmEng and detail some of their main characteristics. For this purpose, we divide the USA up into three main accent areas: the South, the General American area, and the North-east. As we shall see, most of the differences have to do with vowels rather than consonants.

3.3.1.   The South

The area of the USA that Americans refer to as The South is in fact the south-eastern area of the United States. Linguistically, this large area can be divided approximately into two sub-regions: the Lower South and the Inland South.

Map No. 3.   *Regional varieties of educated North American English*

Key   GENERAL AMERICAN: NORTHEASTERN:
       Western   Eastern New England
       Northern   New York City
       Midland
       Central Eastern   CANADIAN:
                                General Canadian
       SOUTHERN: Maritime
       Inland Southern
       Lower Southern   NEWFOUNDLAND

3.3.1.1.   Lower Southern

This area consists of eastern Virginia, eastern North Carolina, eastern South Carolina, northern Florida, southern Alabama, Mississippi, Louisiana and south-eastern Texas. Note that much of the southernmost part of Florida was settled by English speakers only relatively recently and generally has accents of a mixed type more closely resembling those of the West (see 3.3.2.2.), although the older accent of Key West has some Bahamian or Caribbean features.

While there is very considerable regional variation within this area, the major features of the Lower Southern accent are as follows:

1. As far as rhoticity is concerned, the position is rather complicated, but, to simplify somewhat, we can say that, generally, Lower Southern accents are non-rhotic, i.e. they lack non-prevocalic /r/ in words such as *cart* and *car* (see 2.1.3.). Many coastal Lower Southern accents are so non-rhotic, in fact, that, like SAfEng (2.2.3.2.), they lack linking and intrusive /r/ as well as non-prevocalic /r/. It is probable that the loss of /r/ was the result of this innovation from England being diffused outwards in post-settlement times from major East Coast ports such as Charleston.

2. The vowels /ɪ/, /ɛ/, /æ/ often take a [ə] offglide in many stressed monosyllables. At its most extreme, this process of 'breaking', as it is known, can give pronunciations such as *bid* [bɪjəd], *bed* [bejəd], *bad* [bæijəd].

3. The vowel /ai/ is often a monophthong of the type [a:], as in *high* [ha:]. In some parts of The South, this monophthong only occurs word-finally and before voiced consonants, while a diphthongal variant occurs before voiceless consonants, as in *night time* [naɪt ta:m].

4. The /ei/ and /ou/ diphthongs tend to have first elements rather more open than elsewhere in North America. These broad diphthongs thus resemble those of AusNZEng, as well as those of southern England.

5. The vowels /ɪ/ and /ɛ/ are not distinct before a nasal consonant, so that words such as *pin* and *pen* are identical.

6. The verb forms *isn't*, *wasn't* are often pronounced with /d/ rather than /z/: /ɪdnt ~ ɪdn/. There is an increasing tendency to use /d/ rather than /z/ in the word *business* also.

3.3.1.2.   Inland Southern

Inland Southern accents are found in West Virginia, Kentucky, Tennessee, western Virginia, western North Carolina, western South Carolina, northern Georgia, northern Alabama, Arkansas, south-western Missouri, Oklahoma, and most of Texas. They include the Appalachian and Ozark mountain varieties. These accents share with the Lower South most of the features cited under 3.3.1.1. above except that they are typically, if sometimes variably, rhotic. This is presumably because these areas were less susceptible to influence from London as a result of being further away from the East Coast ports.

3.3.1.3.   Black varieties

Many Black Americans, wherever they come from in the United States, have accents which closely resemble those of White speakers from the Lower South, although they are not necessarily identical. The reason for this is that, until the abolition of slavery in the United States, most Americans of African origin were located in the Southern plantation and slave-owning states. On moving to northern and western areas of the USA, Black speakers naturally took their southern accents with them, and subsequent relatively low levels of contact between Black and White Americans have meant that many originally southern features have been maintained in Black speech. Current research suggests that this social separation is also having the consequence that, in the Northern accent area, Black speakers are by and large not participating in the Northern Cities Chain Shift (see 3.3.2.4. below), and that the innovations cited in section 3.3.2.1. below are also almost entirely confined to White speech. (For more on Black varieties, see 6.4.)

3.3.2. General American

General American is a term which is quite widely used by American linguists to describe those American accents—the majority—which do not have marked regional north-eastern or southern characteristics. There are, however, a number of important regional differences within this accent type, which is hardly surprising in view of the vast geographical area it covers.

3.3.2.1. Central Eastern

The Central Eastern area was the area that we discussed at the beginning of this chapter (3.1., 3.2.). In broad outline, the type of vowel system that we discussed in 3.1. is typical of the modern educated USEng accents that are found in south-eastern New York State, most of New Jersey away from New York City, eastern Pennsylvania, Delaware and Maryland. However, we can add a little detail to our earlier description by noting that the vowel system we described in 3.1. is currently being affected by a number of innovations that are altering its character somewhat. These innovations are most apparent in the accents of urban areas and, naturally enough, in the speech of younger people. They include the following:

1. The vowels /ɛ/, /æ/, /ɑ/ are involved in the *Northern Cities Chain Shift*. For an explanation of this phenomenon, see 3.3.2.4.
2. The vowel /ei/ as in *bay* is becoming an increasingly narrow diphthong, with the first element becoming closer, e.g. [e̞ɪ] rather

than [ẹɪ]. This change is the exact opposite of the change affecting this diphthong in the south of England and in AusNZSAfEng, where the diphthong is getting wider. It also has the effect of distancing accents which have this innovation from accents in the American South (see 3.3.1.), where wide diphthongs are usual.

3.   The vowel /ai/ is undergoing a change such that the allophones that occur before voiceless consonants are increasingly different from those that occur elsewhere (cf. 3.3.1. and 3.4.1.). What is happening is that the first element of the diphthong in these contexts is increasingly being raised in the direction of [ə], giving pronunciations such as *night time* [nəɪt taɪm].

4.   The vowel /u/ as in *boot* is becoming increasingly fronted from [u:] in the direction of [ʉ:] (see also 2.1.1., 2.1.2.).

5.   The vowel /ou/ of *boat* is acquiring a fronter first element, although it is not yet as advanced as the [øʉ] that is found in some forms of EngEng RP (see 2.1.1.).

3.3.2.2.   Western

This area comprises the western states of Washington, Oregon, California, Nevada, Idaho, Utah, Arizona, Montana, Wyoming, Colorado, Arizona, North Dakota and South Dakota. This is an extremely large area, and of course its accents are by no means uniform. In particular, urban speech can often be distinguished from rural speech, with urban varieties being a good deal more innovating. The innovations cited for the Central Eastern area (3.3.2.1.), for instance, are much in evidence in this area also, but they are much more typical of younger speakers in places such as San Francisco, Los Angeles, Seattle and Denver than they are of older speakers in rural Wyoming or Montana.

The Northern Cities Chain Shift (see 3.3.2.4.) is not found in this area. Otherwise, the vowel phonology of this area is identical to that of the Central Eastern area (3.1., 3.3.2.1.), with the two following exceptions:

1.   The vowel /ɔ/ of *caught* is gradually disappearing in that it is increasingly becoming merged with the vowel /ɑ/ of *cot*, so that pairs of words such as *taught* and *tot*, *sought* and *sot* are pronounced the same. In the Western area this is a change which is currently in progress, and the merger is thus more apparent in the speech of younger than of older speakers. In certain other regions of North America, this merger has already been completed (see 3.3.2.3., 3.3.3.1., 3.4.1.).

2.   The vowel /æ/ of *bad* is merged with /ε/ before an /r/ which

comes between two syllables, so that *marry* is identical with *merry* [mɛɹi], and *carry* rhymes with *cherry*. This is true of all the General American accents except Central Eastern and is part of a wider pattern in which, in most General American accents, other vowels are also merged before /r/ in words of more than one syllable:

(a) /iː/ and /ɪ/ may be merged before /r/, so that *mirror* and *nearer* are perfect rhymes.

(b) /ɛ/ and /ei/ may be merged before /r/, so that *merry* and *Mary* are pronounced identically. This means that if an accent also has the *merry–marry* merger, then *merry*, *Mary* and *marry* are all pronounced the same.

(c) /ʌ/ and /ə/ may be merged before /r/, so that *hurry* and *furry* are perfect rhymes.

(d) /ɑ/ may be replaced by /ɔ/ or /ou/ before /r/, so that *horrid* has the same initial syllable as *hoary*, and *horrible* rhymes with *deplorable*. This is not a total merger, however, since /ɑ/ still occurs in this position in a small number of words such as *borrow*, *sorrow*, *sorry*, as well as in loan-words such as *sari*, i.e. *sorry* and *sari* are both pronounced /sɑri/ and do not rhyme with *quarry*, which follows the majority pattern, /kwɔri/.

These mergers can all be heard from the second American speaker on the recording.

We should also note that:

3.   Words such as *new*, *nude*, *tune*, *student*, *duke*, *due*, which in many other accents of English have /njuː-/, /tju-/, /dju-/, lack /j/ in these accents, giving pronunciations such as *tune* /tun/, *duke* /duk/.

3.3.2.3.   Midland

The Midland area consists of Nebraska, Kansas, western Iowa, most of Missouri, southern Illinois, southern Indiana, southern Ohio and south-western Pennsylvania. In broad outline, the phonology of this area is identical to that of the Western area (3.3.2.2.), except that the accents of south-western Pennsylvania and eastern Ohio have carried the *cot–caught* merger through to completion. Additionally, however, educated speakers from this area may also retain some features typical of the older rural dialects of the area. Notable amongst these is the behaviour of the vowels /ɪ/, /ɛ/, /æ/, /ʊ/, /ʌ/, /ɑ/, /ɔ/ where they occur before the fricatives /š/ and /ž/:

(a) words such as *fish* may be pronounced with /i/, i.e. /fiš/, identical to *fiche*;

(b) words such as *push* may be pronounced with /u/, i.e. /puš/, rhyming with *douche*;
(c) words such as *special* may be pronounced with /ei/, i.e. /speišəl/, identical to *spatial*;
(d) words such as *mash* may be pronounced with a vowel of the type [æɪ], i.e. [mæɪš];
(e) words wuch as *hush* may be pronounced with a vowel of the type [əɪ], i.e. [həɪš].

Most noticeable, however, is the fact that words such as *wash* may be pronounced with /ɔr/, i.e. /wɔrš/, rhyming with *Porsche*.

3.3.2.4.   Northern

This area is focused on the major northern cities of Minneapolis, Chicago, Detroit, Cleveland and Buffalo, and covers Minnesota, Wisconsin, northern Illinois, northern Indiana, northern Ohio, northern Pennsylvania, north-western New York and west Vermont. The accents of this area are in most respects broadly identical to those of the Western area. One major difference, however, is that they are currently undergoing a process of change which American linguists have labelled the *Northern Cities Chain Shift*. This relatively recent set of innovations involves the vowels /ɛ/, /æ/ and /ɑ/ in a series of linked movements in vowel space.

1.   /ɑ/ is moving forwards to take up a front vowel position [æ ~ a] closer to the original position of /æ/. This can lead speakers from other accent areas to misinterpret, say, *John* as *Jan*.
2.   /æ/ is, in its turn, lengthening and moving upwards through [ɛ:] to [e:] and even diphthongizing to [eə] or [ɪə]. This can lead, at its most advanced, to speakers from other areas misinterpreting, say, *Ann* as *Ian*. The degree of raising and diphthongizing of this vowel varies considerably from place to place, word to word, and phonological environment to phonological environment, with the following consonant being the most important determining factor: e.g. *man* may be [mɪən] but *mat* [mɛət]. Buffalo in New York State is said to be the place where this particular change is at its most advanced.
3.   /ɛ/, presumably in order to move out of the way of /æ/ as it rises, is retracting and becoming a more central vowel closer in quality to /ʌ/, so that *best* may sound very like *bust*.

3.3.3.   Northeastern

This accent area can be divided into two major subdivisions: Eastern New England and New York City.

3.3.3.1. Eastern New England

A very distinct accent, instantly recognizable to other Americans, is associated with the Eastern New England area. This region centres on the city of Boston and includes the states of Maine, New Hampshire, Rhode Island, eastern Vermont, eastern Connecticut and eastern and central Massachusetts. This accent resembles the accents of England more than any other American accent, and there are a number of phonetic similarities with AusNZEng. This resemblance is due to continuing close links between the port of Boston and London in post-settlement times and the resultant importation of originally southern English features into this area of the United States.

Features of Eastern New England speech which distinguish it from Central Eastern (3.1., 3.3.2.1.) and which are due to historical influences from EngEng include the following:

1. The accents of the area are non-rhotic and have both linking and intrusive /r/ (see 2.1.3.). They share with EngEng and the Southern Hemisphere varieties the vowels /ɪə/, /ɛə/, /ʊə/, /ɜ:/ of *peer*, *pair*, *poor*, *bird*. In regions further away from Boston, however, /r/ does occur after /ə/ in items such as *bird* and *butter*. In the speech of younger speakers, moreover, non-prevocalic /r/ is beginning to be reintroduced as a result of influence from the mainstream American norm.
2. Like EngEng, these accents have an additional vowel /a:/, which is used in words such as *bard*, as well as in words such as *calm* and *father* and words such as *dance* and *path*. This vowel is phonetically a rather front [a:]. This feature, too, is rather recessive, with younger speakers increasingly favouring mainstream American forms.
3. The vowel of *pot*, *horrid*, etc. is a rounded vowel /ɒ/ rather than the more usual American unrounded /ɑ/.

The other distinctive Eastern New England feature is:

4. The *cot–caught* merger has been completed in these accents, both sets of words having /ɒ/ (see 3.3.2.2.). Because /ɔ/ is lacking, and because these accents are also non-rhotic, items such as *port* also have the /ɒ/ vowel, so that *sot*, *sought* and *sort* can all be pronounced the same, which is not true of any EngEng accent.
5. Younger speakers in Boston and other urban areas also have the Northern Cities Chain Shift (see 3.3.2.4.).

3.3.3.2.   New York City

New York is the largest city in the United States, and indeed in the whole of the American continent. It too has a very distinctive accent, which is also found in the immediately adjoining areas of New York State, Connecticut and New Jersey. This distinctiveness can be ascribed in part, like that of the Boston area, to the city's role as a port with close links with England at earlier periods, but it is also due in part to considerable immigration by speakers of Yiddish, Irish, Irish English, Italian and other European languages, as well as to independent developments. Sociolinguistically, there is more social stratification on the British model in the accents of New York City than anywhere else in North America, with upper social class accents having many fewer local features than lower class accents. Characteristic features of New York English pronunciation include the following:

1.   New York City English, like that of Boston, is non-rhotic, and linking and intrusive /r/ are usual. As a consequence, the local accent shares with RP and the other non-rhotic accents the vowels /ɪə/, /ɛə/, /ʊə/, /ɜ:/ as in *peer, pair, poor, bird*. However, as in the Boston area, younger speakers are now becoming increasingly rhotic, especially amongst higher social class groups.

2.   Like Boston, New York also has an additional vowel corresponding to RP /a:/. In New York, however, it is phonetically /ɑə/. This vowel occurs in words such as *bard* as well as in *calm, father*, as in Boston; but unlike Boston, it does not occur in *dance, path*, which have /æ/ instead.

3.   The vowel /ɜ:/ has a typical New York pronunciation where it occurs before a consonant in the same word, as in *bird, girl*. This is a diphthong of the type [ɜɪ]: [bɜɪd]. This was formerly a pronunciation used by all New Yorkers, but it is now most usual in lower class speech, and is not so frequent in the speech of younger people. In word-final position, as in *her*, [ɜ:] occurs.

4.   Unlike the Eastern New England accent, words such as *pot, horrid* have the more usual American unrounded vowel /ɑ/.

5.   Unlike the Eastern New England accent, the New York accent does not lack the vowel /ɔ/, and so *cot* and *caught* are distinct, and *sot* /sɑt/ is distinct from *sought* and *sort* /sɔt/. The /ɔ/ vowel of *caught, sought, talk, paw, long, off, port, sort*, etc., however, has a distinctive New York pronunciation which is typically a rather close and often diphthongized vowel of the type [oə] or even [ʊə], as in *off* [ʊəf].

6.   The distinctively New York /ai/ vowel of *buy, night, ride* has a back first element, not unlike that of Cockney or AusNZEng, of the type [ɑɪ] or even [ɒɪ].

7. Many New Yorkers have pronunciations of /θ/ and /ð/ as dental stops [t] and [d]. In the case of /ð/, this can lead to a merger with /d/, so that *then* and *den* are possible homophones. This feature, however, is not so common in educated speech.

8. The accents of New York City are also involved in the Northern Cities Chain Shift (see 3.3.2.4.).

3.4. The pronunciation of Canadian English

As far as phonology is concerned, Canadian English can be divided into three main types: General, Maritime and Newfoundland.

3.4.1. General Canadian

This area covers most of English-speaking Canada, from Victoria and Vancouver in the west to Toronto, Ottawa and the English-speaking minority in Montreal in the east. The vowel system of this type of CanEng is identical with that of the Western area of the United States, although it does not have any of the innovations listed under 3.3.2.1., but with the following additional features:

1. The most distinctive feature of Canadian English, and the one which Americans use in spotting Canadian speakers, is the phenomenon known to linguists as *Canadian Raising*. This refers to the fact that, before voiceless consonants, the diphthongs /ai/ and /au/ have allophones with raised central first elements which differ considerably from those which they have elsewhere. This gives pronunciations such as *night time* [nəit taim] and *out loud* [əut laud]. As we saw in section 3.3.2.1., raised variants of /ai/ before voiceless consonants are now becoming common in USEng also, so that it is the raised allophone of /au/ in words such as *out, house, mouth* which is now the most distinctively Canadian feature. Canadian Raising can be heard on the recording in *night, bout, about*.

2. The loss of the vowel /ɔ/ and the merger of words such as *cot* and *caught* as /kɑt/ (see also 3.3.2.1., 3.3.2.3., 3.3.3.1.) is complete in all forms of General Canadian English.

3. Unlike General American, Canadian English has /ou/ in words such as *borrow, sorrow, sorry. Sorry* thus rhymes with *hoary*. Loan-words such as *sari* have /ɑ/.

4. The diphthongs /ei/ and /ou/ of *bay* and *boat* are very narrow. (The narrow pronunciation of /ei/ is a well-established feature of CanEng and not an innovation, as it is in some forms of USEng—see 3.3.2.1.)

5.   Although American cities such as Detroit and Buffalo are only a short distance from the Canadian border, the Northern Cities Chain Shift (see 3.3.2.4.) is not found in CanEng. Indeed, the vowel /æ/ of *bad* and *bat* may be very open, in some cases approaching [a]. Note too that some foreign words spelt with *a*, such as *pasta*, are pronounced with /æ/, as in EngEng, rather than /ɑ/, as in USEng.

3.4.2.   Maritime

The Maritimes are the eastern coastal provinces of Prince Edward Island, Nova Scotia and New Brunswick, which are geographically separated from the rest of English-speaking Canada by French-speaking Quebec. In this long-settled area, there is quite a large amount of regional variation. Its most notable characteristic with respect to General Canadian English, however, is that it lacks Canadian Raising, so that /ai/ and /au/ tend to have rather open first elements in all environments.

3.4.3.   Newfoundland

The large island of Newfoundland has been part of Canada only since 1949, but it was settled by English speakers as early as the 16th century. There is some regional variation; in particular, some areas have accents more like those of the south-west of England, and others have accents more closely resembling those of the south of Ireland. There is also considerable social variation, with large differences between local dialects and more standard forms of speech. Educated speakers of Newfoundland English have phonological systems which are very similar to those of SIrEng (see Chapter 5), although there are phonetic differences. Important features are the following:

1.   Like the Maritimes, Newfoundland does not have the allophonic differentiation of /ai/ and /au/ typical of Canadian Raising. Unlike the Maritimes, however, it has central first elements to these diphthongs in *all* phonological environments, giving pronunciations such as *night time* [nəɪt təɪm], *out loud* [əʊt ləʊd].
2.   The vowels of *cot* and *caught* remain distinct.

3.5. Non-systematic differences between North American English and English English pronunciation

Many of the differences between 'American' and 'English' varieties of English involve the pronunciation of individual or small groups of words. We now give some indication of these.

1. We list first a few individual words which differ in no particularly predictable way between USEng and EngEng (note that CanEng often uses the EngEng variant; stress is the same for both pronunciations of these words):

	USEng	*EngEng*
charade	/šəreɪd/	/šɑrɑːd/
cordial	/kɔrǰəl/	/kɔːdiːəl/
deterrent	/dɪtərənt/	/dɪtɛrənt/
herb	/ərb/	/hɜːb/
leisure	/ližər/	/lɛžə/ (also US)
lever	/lɛvər/	/liːvə/ (also US)
privacy	/praivəsi/	/prɪvəsɪ/ ~ /praivəsɪ/
route	/rut/ ~ /raut/	/ruːt/
schedule	/skɛǰəl/	/šɛǰuːl/
shone	/šoun/	/šɒn/
tomato	/təmeitou/	/təmɑːtou/
vase	/veis/ ~ /veiz/	/vɑːz/

2. NAmEng *aluminum* /əlúmənəm/ differs both in pronunciation and (as a reflection of this) in spelling from EngEng *aluminium* /æluːmínjəm/.

3. *Either, neither* can have either /iː/:/i/ or /ai/ on both sides of the Atlantic, but in educated speech /iðər/ is more common in USEng, /aiðə/ in EngEng.

4. A number of words spelled with *er* have /ər/ in NAmEng corresponding to /ɑː/ ~ /ɑr/ elsewhere: *clerk*, NAmEng /klərk/, EngEng /klɑːk/. Similarly *derby, Berkshire*.

5. *Of, what, was* have /ʌ/ in NAmEng, /ɒ/ elsewhere. Thus *what* rhymes with *but* in NAmEng but with *not* in EngEng.

6. *Apparatus, data, status* can be pronounced with either stressed /æ/ or /ei/ in NAmEng, but only with stressed /ei/ in EngEng.

7. Words like *fertile, hostile, juvenile, missile, mobile, sterile* have final /ail/ in EngEng. In NAmEng, the final syllable may be either /ail/ or /əl/. Note that *docile* is /dousail/ in EngEng, /dɑsəl/ in NAmEng.

8. The prefixes *anti-* and *semi-* have final /ɪ/ ~ /iː/ in EngEng. In

addition to these pronunciations, NAmEng also has final /ai/ for these prefixes.

9.   *Tunisia* is pronounced /tunížə/ in NAmEng but /tjuːníziːə/ in EngEng. *Asia* has /ž/ in NAmEng, /š/ or /ž/ in EngEng.

3.6.   Stress differences

1.   In a number of words of foreign, especially French, origin, NAmEng tends to have stress on the final syllable while EngEng does not. Thus:

	NAmEng	*EngEng*
attaché	/ætæšéi/	/ətǽšei/
ballet	/bæléi/	/bǽlei/
baton	/bətán/	/bǽtɒn/
beret	/bəréi/	/bέrɪ/ ~ /bέrei/
debris	/dəbrí/	/débriː/

2.   There are a number of words having first-syllable stress in NAmEng but with stress elsewhere in EngEng. A few examples are:

	NAmEng	*EngEng*
address	/ǽdres/ ~ /ədrέs/	/ədrέs/
adult	/ǽdʌlt/ ~ /ǽdəlt/	/ədʌ́lt/ ~ /ǽdʌlt/
cigarette	/sígərɛt/ ~ /sɪgərét/	/sɪgərét/
inquiry	/íŋkwərɪ/ ~ /ɪŋkwáɪrɪ/	/ɪŋkwáɪərɪ/
magazine	/mǽgəzin/ ~ /mægəzín/	/mægəzíːn/
margarine	/márǰərən/	/mɑːǰəríːn/
research	/rísərč/	/rəsέːč/

Note that *research*, as a noun, is now increasingly pronounced with first-syllable stress in EngEng.

3.   A number of compound words have acquired stress on the first element of NAmEng but retain stress on the second element in EngEng. The compounds include *weekend, hotdog, New Year, ice cream*.

4.   Many polysyllabic words ending in *-ory* or *-ary* normally have stress on the first or second syllable in EngEng, with the penultimate syllable being reduced. In NAmEng there is, in addition, secondary stress on the penultimate syllable:

	NAmEng	*EngEng*
auditory	/ɔ́dɪtɔ̀ri/	/ɔ́ːdɪtrɪ/
commentary	/káməntὲri/	/kɒ́məntrɪ/
dictionary	/díkšənὲri/	/díkšənrɪ/
lavatory	/lǽvətɔ̀ri/	/lǽvətrɪ/
secretary	/sékrətὲri/	/sékrətrɪ/

In EngEng, partially reduced pronunciations are also possible, but there is never secondary stress on the penultimate syllable: *dictionary* /díkšənərɪ/.

In a number of words of this set, the primary stress is also located differently:

	USEng	*EngEng*
laboratory	/lǽbrətɔ̀ri/	/ləbɒ́rətrɪ/
corollary	/kɑ́rəlèri/	/kərɒ́lərɪ/
capillary	/kǽpɪlèri/	/kəpílərɪ/
ancillary	/ǽnsɪlèri/	/ænsílərɪ/

(Note that all words discussed here have at least four syllables in NAmEng: i.e. none of the above remarks applies to, e.g. *vagary*.)

The same type of difference also appears in a number of words ending in -*mony*:

	NAmEng	*EngEng*
matrimony	/mǽtrɪmòuni/	/mǽtrɪmənɪ/
testimony	/téstɪmòuni/	/téstɪmənɪ/

5.   Many place names (and family names derived from them) demonstrate more stress and vowel reduction in EngEng than in NAmEng:

	NAmEng	*EngEng*
Birmingham	/bɜ́rmiŋhæ̀m/	/bɜ́ːmɪŋəm/
Cunningham	/kʌ́nɪŋhæ̀m/	/kʌ̀nɪŋəm/
Norfolk	/nɔ́rfouk/	/nɔ́ːfək/
Norwich	/nɔ́rwɪč/	/nɒ́rɪǰ/
Portsmouth	/pɔ́rtsmòuθ/	/pɔ́ːtsməθ/

3.7.   Further differences between American English and Canadian English pronunciation

In a few respects, Canadian pronunciation follows EngEng rather than USEng:

1.   *been* is usually /bɪn/ in USEng, but occasionally /biːn/ in CanEng as, more usually, in EngEng.
2.   *again(st)* is usually /əgɛ́n/ in USEng. This pronunciation is also used in Canada and the UK, but in CanEng and EngEng it can also be /əgeín/.
3.   As mentioned above, *corollary, capillary* are stressed on the first syllable in USEng, with secondary stress on the penultimate syllable. CanEng follows EngEng in having the stress on the second syllable.
4.   CanEng has *shone* as /šan/, never /šoun/ as in USEng.
5.   Some CanEng speakers have *tomato* as /təmætou/.

4

English and North American English: grammatical, orthographical and lexical differences

At the level of educated speech and writing, there are relatively few differences in grammar and spelling between EngEng and NAmEng; those which do exist tend to be fairly trivial when considered from the point of view of mutual understanding. Vocabulary differences, on the other hand, are very numerous and are capable of causing varying degrees of comprehension problems. Each of these three areas will be discussed in turn below.

It should be noted that we treat EngEng and NAmEng, often, as if they were two entirely homogeneous and separate varieties. This makes the presentation of the facts more straightforward, but it does obscure, to a certain extent, the fact that there is regional variation, even in Standard English, in the two areas. There is also considerable influence of the one variety on the other, particularly of NAmEng on EngEng; thus, what is NAmEng usage for older English people may be perfectly normal EngEng usage for younger English people.

4.1. Grammatical differences

In this section we will discuss differences both in morphology and syntax. We will also note some differences in frequency of use of certain constructions which occur in both varieties.

4.1.1. The verb

4.1.1.1. Morphology

1. *Inflectional.* In English, 'regular' verbs are characterized as having two distinct 'principle parts': a present tense form, and a past tense/past participle form which is made by adding *-(e)d* to the present tense form, e.g.:

Present	Past	Past Participle
call	called	called
create	created	created

There are many 'irregular' or 'strong' verbs in English, however, which do not follow this pattern, diverging in a variety of ways, e.g.:

Present	Past	Past Participle
fly	flew	flown
hit	hit	hit
sing	sang	sung
teach	taught	taught

In NAmEng, a number of irregular verbs have become regularized, while remaining irregular in EngEng:

(a) In many instances, it is only the voicing of the past tense morpheme *-(e)d* which has been changed to regularize the verb:

	EngEng	
Present	Past and Past Participle	Past and Past Participle
burn	burnt	burned
dwell	dwelt	dwelled
learn	learnt	learned
smell	smelt	smelled
spell	spelt	spelled
spill	spilt	spilled
spoil	spoilt	spoiled

(b) In some irregular EngEng verbs, there is a vowel change from /i/ in the present to /ɛ/ in the past and past participle forms. The NAmEng forms retain the present tense vowel in the following cases, as well as voicing the ending:

	EngEng	**USEng**
Present	**Past and Past Participle**	**Past and Past Participle**
dream	dreamt /drɛmt/	dreamed /drimd/
kneel	knelt	kneeled
lean	leant	leaned
leap	leapt	leaped

The NAmEng forms are also possible now in EngEng and the EngEng forms may still be found in formal language and poetry in NAmEng.

(c) In a few instances, the NAmEng forms are more irregular than the EngEng forms:

	EngEng	**NAmEng**	
Present	**Past and Past Participle**	**Past**	**Past Participle**
dive	dived	dove	dived
fit	fitted	fit	fitted
sneak	sneaked	snuck	snuck
get	got	got	gotten

NAmEng also uses *dived*, *fitted*, and *sneaked* for the past tense, but the irregular forms are more frequent:

He dove/dived in head first
That suit fit/fitted me last week
He snuck/sneaked around the corner

The past participle *gotten* is not used in EngEng. In NAmEng it was formerly restricted to being used in the sense of 'obtain' or 'acquire':

I've gotten a new car since I last saw you

Now, however, *gotten* can be used in all meanings except for 'have' in NAmEng, e.g.:

We have gotten home late again
We've gotten together every June
We had already gotten off the train when it was hit
They've gotten me into trouble again

but

I've got plenty to eat
I've got the idea now (='I understand')

2.   *Derivational*

(a) One way of making or 'deriving' new verbs is to add a verb-forming suffix or prefix onto a noun or adjective: e.g.

symbol—symbolize, ripe—ripen, frost—defrost. While it is usually the case that the same derivational suffixes are productive in both varieties of English, NAmEng tends perhaps to be more productive in its derivations, i.e. some affixes are used on classes of words or with particular senses of words where they would not be used in EngEng. While many such derived words are considered 'jargon' and not accepted into common use in NAmEng, those which are accepted are often borrowed quickly into EngEng.

Two verb-forming affixes which are somewhat more productive in USEng than EngEng are:

-ify: *citify, humidify, uglify*
-ize: *burglarize, decimalize, hospitalize, rubberize,*
        slenderize

(b) Another way of forming new words is by simply changing a word's grammatical class, e.g. using a noun as a verb. This process is common to both varieties, with innovations spreading rapidly from one to the other. Again, there is more of a tendency to form new words in this way in USEng than in EngEng, e.g.:

Noun	*Verb*
an author	*to author*
a host	*to host* (e.g. *We hosted a reunion last week*)
a sky-rocket	*to sky-rocket* (e.g. *Prices are sky-rocketing this year*)
pressure	*to pressure* (EngEng *to pressurize*)
a room	*to room* (e.g. *I room at that house*)

4.1.1.2. Auxiliaries

An auxiliary verb, as the name implies, does not exist as an independent verb in a sentence but must combine with a lexical verb to form a verb phrase. Different auxiliaries have various functions, such as entering into specific syntactic processes (question formation, negative contraction), expressing aspect (progressive and perfective), and expressing modality (volition, probability, obligation).

1. *Modal auxiliaries.* Several of the modals are used with a different frequency or meaning in NAmEng than in EngEng:

(a) *shall. Shall* is rarely used in NAmEng, except in legal documents or very formal styles, and is replaced by *will* (or *should* in questions with first person subjects). The negative form *shan't* is even rarer in USEng. Both varieties also often use the contracted form *'ll*.

EngEng	NAmEng and EngEng
I shall tell you later	*I will tell you later/I'll tell you later*
Shall I drink this now?	*Should I drink this now?*
I shan't be able to come	*I won't be able to come*

(b) *should*. As well as expressing obligation and tentativeness, *should* in EngEng can also have a hypothetical sense when it occurs in a main clause with a first person subject followed by a conditional clause. This use is mainly restricted to older speakers and writers. In NAmEng (and with younger EngEng speakers), *would* is used instead in such sentences:

(Older) EngEng:	*I should enjoy living here if I could afford to do so*
NAmEng and younger EngEng:	*I would enjoy living here if . . .*

(c) *would*. USEng has two uses for this modal that are much less usual in EngEng. First, *would* can be used in expressing a characteristic or habitual activity in USEng:

When I was young, I would go there every day

In EngEng either the simple past or the verb with the modal *used to* would probably be used (this is also possible in USEng):

$$When\ I\ was\ young,\ I\ \begin{Bmatrix} went \\ used\ to\ go \end{Bmatrix}\ there\ every\ day$$

Second, while in EngEng *would* cannot be used to express a hypothetical state if this is already signalled by the verb or by a conditional clause, in many USEng dialects *would* can be used in this way in informal speech:

USEng only	EngEng and USEng
I wish I would have done it	*I wish I had done it*
If I would have seen one, I would have bought it for you	*If I had seen one, I would have bought it for you*

(This second use of *would* is relatively recent in USEng and is more likely to be encountered in speech than in writing.)

In EngEng, *would* and *will* are often used in a predictive sense, as in:

That will be the postman at the door
That would be the building you want
Would that be High Street over there?

In USEng, it is more common to use the auxiliaries *should* or *must* in such sentences or not to have any auxiliary:

$$That \begin{cases} is \\ should\ be \\ must\ be \end{cases} the\ mailman\ at\ the\ door$$

$$That \begin{cases} is \\ should\ be \end{cases} the\ building\ you\ want$$

Is that High Street over there?

These other forms are also used in EngEng.

(d) *must*. The negative of epistemic *must* is *can't* in southern EngEng:

He must be in—his TV is on
He can't be in—his car has gone

(In the north-west of England, *mustn't* is used rather than *can't*.)

In USEng, the most common negative of epistemic *must* is *must not*. Note that, unlike north-west EngEng, in USEng this cannot be contracted to *mustn't* without changing the meaning of the auxiliary to 'not be allowed':

He must not be in—his car is gone	(epistemic)
You mustn't be in when we arrive	('not allowed')

However, *mustn't* can be epistemic in the past perfect:

He mustn't have been in

Even in such cases, however, the uncontracted form is preferred in USEng.

(e) *use(d) to*. In questioning or negating sentences with the modal *used to*, EngEng can treat *used to* either as an auxiliary, in which case it inverts in questions and receives negation, or as a lexical verb requiring *do* for these constructions:

He used to go there	
Used he to go there?	(auxiliary)
Did he use to go there?	(lexical verb)
He used not to go there	(auxiliary)
He didn't use to go there	(lexical verb)

In USEng, *used to* is treated only as a lexical verb in these constructions, and this is also becoming increasingly the case in EngEng.

(f) *ought to*. USEng rarely uses this auxiliary in questions or negated forms. Instead, *should* is used:

EngEng	USEng
Ought we to eat that?	*Should we eat that?*
(older speakers)	

$You\begin{Bmatrix}ought\ not\\oughtn't\end{Bmatrix}$ *to have said that*   *You shouldn't have said that*

You oughtn't have said that
(rare, formal)

Note that when *ought* is used in USEng in the negative, the *to* is usually deleted.

EngEng also can treat *ought to* as a lexical verb, similar to *used to*, in informal styles. These forms are considered non-standard in USEng:

Did you ought to eat that?
You didn't ought to have said that

(g) *dare* and *need*. Both of these auxiliaries are rare in USEng and usually occur in set phrases, such as:

Need I say more?
Persons under 18 need not apply
I dare say . . .

As with *used to*, USEng treats *dare* and *need* as lexical verbs in negating and questioning. EngEng also has this option:

EngEng (only): *Need you be so rude?*   (auxiliary)
USEng and
EngEng: *Do you need to be so rude?*   (verb)

EngEng (only): *You needn't be so rude!*   (auxiliary)
USEng and
EngEng: *You don't need to be so rude!*   (verb)

EngEng (only): *Dare I tell the truth?*   (auxiliary)
USEng and
EngEng: *Do I dare (to) tell the truth?*   (verb)

EngEng (only): *I daren't tell the truth*   (auxiliary)
USEng and
EngEng: *I don't dare (to) tell the truth*   (verb)

(h) *mayn't*. The contracted form of *may not* is only found in EngEng, and fairly rarely even there.

2.   *do*. The auxiliary *do*, which is empty of meaning, is required in all varieties when constructing question and negative forms of

simple verbs. (*Do you want this? I don't want this.*). It can also be used for polite commands or requests: *Do go on! Do sit down.* This last use is much less common in USEng, where *please* would be used instead.

3. *have, do have* and *have got.* A well-known grammatical difference between EngEng and USEng lies in the differing use of *have, do have* and *have got* to indicate possession. The situation has changed over the past few decades, so that what once were exclusively USEng or EngEng usages are no longer such.

Consider the following sentences:

(i)	*Have you any fresh cod?*	(possess at present)
	I haven't any fresh cod	
(ii)	*Have you got (any) fresh cod?*	(possess at present)
	I haven't got (any) fresh cod	
(iii)	*Do you have (any) fresh cod?*	(possess at present)
	I don't have (any) fresh cod	
(iv)	*Do you have fresh cod?*	(usually possess)
	I don't have fresh cod	

In the (i) sentences, the lexical verb *have* functions as an auxiliary (i.e. it does not require the auxiliary *do* for question and negation; also, it can contract, as in *We've some fresh cod today*). Such sentences are usual, if somewhat formal or older, in EngEng, but are rare in USEng. Sentences like (ii) are usual in both varieties in more informal styles. Sentences of the (iii) type are the most usual ways of constructing question and negative forms indicating possession in USEng and are now also used in EngEng, although not long ago *do you have* could only be used in the habitual (iv) sense in EngEng. Sentences like those in (iv) are widely used in EngEng to express habitual possession but are not usual in USEng, where a paraphrase such as *Do you usually/ever have fresh cod* would be preferred. Thus an exchange like the following would make perfect sense to an EngEng speaker but might puzzle a USEng speaker:

Q *Have you (got) any fresh cod?*
A *No, I haven't*
Q *Do you have fresh cod?*
A *Yes, but we've already sold it all today*

In the past tense, the situation is more complicated.

(v)	*Had you any money at that time?*	(possessed)
	I hadn't any money at that time	
(vi)	*Had you got any money at that time?*	(possessed, not
	I hadn't got any money at that time	acquired)

(vii)   *Did you have any money at that time?*   (habitually, or
    I didn't have any money at that time   possessed at
                                          specific time)

The (v) sentences are used only by older EngEng speakers. The (vi) sentences are usual in EngEng but not usual in USEng. The (vii) sentences are widely used in both varieties.

Answers to the question types in (i) to (iii) above also differ between USEng and EngEng. In both varieties, the answer to a yes–no question can consist of just a subject and auxiliary(ies), the rest of the verb phrase being understood:

Did you go often?   Yes, I did
Have you seen them?   Yes, I have
Were you travelling a long time?   Yes, we were
Would they have done that?   Yes, they would (have)

However, for all of (i) to (iii), the EngEng reply would be *I have* or *I haven't* (even in (iii) where the auxiliary *do* is present), and the USEng reply would be *I do* or *I don't* (even in (i) and (ii) where the auxiliary is *have*) e.g.:

EngEng	**USEng**
Q *Do you have any fresh cod?*	Q *Have you got fresh cod?*
A *Yes, I have*	A *Yes, I do*

4.   In NAmEng, uninverted response questions of the type:

John went home
He did?

I'll do it
You will?

are very common, and indicate only mild surprise or interest. In EngEng inverted response questions such as:

John went home
Did he?

I'll do it
Will you?

are really the only possibility, although the NAmEng forms may be possible for some EngEng speakers as an indication of strong surprise.

4.1.1.3. Verb phrase substitutions with *do*

In both EngEng and NAmEng, lexically empty *do* can substitute for a simple finite verb phrase which is the repetition of a verb phrase from the same or preceding sentence. *Do* is inflected for tense and person in such substitutions, e.g.:

John likes classical music and Mary does too (=likes classical music)

John left work early today
Oh? He did yesterday, too (=left work early)

However, EngEng and NAmEng differ in the use of *do* substitution with an auxiliary. In EngEng *do* substitution can occur after most auxiliaries, *do* being inflected for tense (but not person). In NAmEng, *do* cannot be used in such instances. Instead of substitution, a deletion process is used whereby both the verb and its object are deleted. Also, if there are two aspectual auxiliaries, the second (in general) can be deleted. EngEng can also employ this deletion process. The following examples illustrate this:

Context	*Do-substitution* (EngEng only)	*Deletion* (Both NAm and EngEng)
Did he pass his exams?	*Yes, he did do*	*Yes, he did*
Have you cleaned your room?	*Yes, I have done*	*Yes, I have*
I haven't read this yet	*but I will do*	*but I will*
Will you have finished by next Monday?	*Yes, I will have done*	{ *Yes, I will have* { *Yes, I will*
I haven't bought one	*but I may do*	*but I may*
Will he come with us tonight?	*He might do*	*He might*
I haven't thrown them out	*but I should do*	*but I should*
Couldn't you do that later?	*Yes, we could do*	*Yes, we could*
Would you have recognized him?	*No, I wouldn't have done*	{ *No, I wouldn't have* *No, I wouldn't* (informal)

There are certain constructions even within finite verb phrases in which *do*-substitution cannot occur or are unusual in EngEng: when the passive voice is used; when the progressive aspect is used; and when 'semi-auxiliaries' (*happen to*, *be going to*, etc.) are used. (The acceptability of *do*-substitution with progressive aspect, semi-auxiliaries, and negated auxiliaries is also subject to regional variation in EngEng.) Where *do*-substitution is not acceptable, deletion occurs:

Context	*Do-substitution*	*Deletion*
Passive Voice	*(EngEng only)*	*(NAmEng and EngEng)*
Were you fired?	**Yes, I was done*	*Yes, I was*
Have you been injured?	**Yes, I have been done*	*{ Yes, I have been* *Yes, I have*
Progressive Aspect		
Are you working now?	*?Yes, I am doing*	*Yes, I am*
Will you be gardening tomorrow?	*?Yes, we will be doing*	*{ Yes, we will be* *Yes, we will*
He must have been driving home	*?Yes, he must have been doing*	*{ Yes, he must have been* *Yes, he must have*
Semi-auxiliary		
I haven't written to her yet	*?but I'm going to do*	*but I'm going to*
We didn't mean to fall in love	*?We just happened to do*	*We just happened to*
Negated Auxiliary		
I wanted to go	*?but I couldn't do*	*but I couldn't*
Have you read that yet?	*No, I haven't done*	*No, I haven't*
We stayed out late	*but we shouldn't have done*	*but we shouldn't have*

4.1.1.4.   Verb phrases

1.   Certain verbs, like *give*, *show*, *tell*, *bring* take two objects, a direct object (DO) and an indirect object (IO). The indirect object, which is semantically a 'recipient', can occur with a preposition (usually *to* or *for*) after the DO, or it can occur before the DO without a preposition:

John gave the book to Mary
          DO   IO

John gave Mary the book
       IO   DO

When the DO is a pronoun, USEng requires the order DO + preposition + IO, as does southern EngEng:

USEng and southern EngEng
John gave it to Mary
*John gave Mary it

When both the DO and IO are pronouns, EngEng allows both orderings. It also permits deletion of the preposition in the first pattern, although this construction is somewhat old-fashioned except in northern EngEng:

USEng	**Southern EngEng**	**Northern EngEng**
John gave it to me	*John gave it to me*	*John gave it to me*
	John gave me it	*John gave me it*
		John gave it me

When comparing passive and active versions of a sentence, it can be seen that the DO of the active sentence corresponds to the subject (S) of the passive, and the S of the active corresponds to the object of a *by* prepositional phrase (OP) of the passive (or is deleted):

Active: *John hit Mary*
      S   DO
Passive: *Mary was hit (by John)*
       S   OP

In passive versions of double-object verbs like those above, there are usually two possible nouns which can be subjects—the DO or the IO of the active version:

The book was given to Mary by John
Mary was given the book by John

In USEng, when the active DO is used as the passive subject, the IO must occur with a preposition:

The book was given to Mary by John
*The book was given Mary by John

Both sentences are allowed in EngEng. Also, in some varieties of USEng, when the DO is a pronoun, the IO cannot be used as a passive subject:

*Mary was given it by John

Again, however, this is possible in EngEng.

2.   The verb *like* may take an infinitive (or infinitive clause) or an *-ing* participle (or clause) as its object:

Infinitive:	*I like to skate*	*I like to photograph animals in the wild*
-ing Participle:	*I like skating*	*I like photographing animals in the wild*

In EngEng the *-ing* participle construction is preferred.

When the object of *like* is a clause and the subject of that clause is not coreferential with the subject of *like*, then a *for ... to* infinitive can be used in USEng. The normal *to* infinitive is usually used in such instances in EngEng.

EngEng and USEng	**USEng**
We'd like you to do this now	*We'd like for you to do this now*

3.   In EngEng the copular verbs *seem*, *act*, *look* and *sound* can be followed directly by an indefinite noun phrase. In USEng, these verbs must be followed first by the preposition *like*; *seem* can also be followed by the infinitive *to be*:

EngEng	**USEng/EngEng**
It seemed a long time	*It seemed like a long time*
He seems an intelligent man	*He seems to be an intelligent man*
John acted a real fool	*John acted like a real fool*
That house looks a nice one	*That house looks like a nice one*
That sounds a bad idea	*That sounds like a bad idea*

4.   *Come* and *go* may be followed by another verb either in a *to* + infinitive construction or conjoined by *and*:

We are coming to see you soon

He went $\begin{Bmatrix} and\ fixed \\ to\ fix \end{Bmatrix}$ *it yesterday*

When *come* and *go* are uninflected (both for tense and person), the *to* or *and* are often dropped in USEng, but not usually in EngEng:

EngEng/NAmEng	**USEng**
We'll come to see you soon	*We'll come see you soon*
Go and fix it now	*Go fix it now*
Can I come and have a cup of coffee with you?	*Can I come have a cup of coffee with you?*

NAmEng is also much more likely than EngEng to delete *to* after *help* when followed by another verb, even when *help* is inflected:

EngEng/NAmEng   **NAmEng**
I'll help to mow the lawn   *I'll help mow the lawn*
John helped us to mow the lawn   *John helped us mow the lawn*

5.   When the verb *order* is followed by a passive verb, *to be* is often deleted in USEng, leaving the passive participle:

EngEng/USEng   **USEng**
He ordered the men to be   *He ordered the men evacuated*
  evacuated
We ordered that to be done   *We ordered that done*
  immediately   *immediately*

6.   The verb *want* can be followed directly by the adverbs *in* and *out* in USEng. In EngEng *want* must be followed first by an infinitive:

EngEng   **USEng**

I wanted $\begin{Bmatrix} to\ come\ in \\ to\ be\ let\ in \end{Bmatrix}$ *I wanted in*

  The dog wants to go out   *The dog wants out*

Also, *want* can be used in the sense of 'need' in EngEng with an inanimate subject:

The house wants painting

This is not possible in NAmEng.

7.   The verb *wonder* can be followed by a finite clause introduced by *if*, *whether*, or a *wh*-relative pronoun in both varieties:

I wonder if/whether he is coming
I wonder where he went

In EngEng, *wonder* can also be followed by a clause introduced by *that* (*that* is actually optional). In USEng, a periphrastic construction, or a different verb, is used instead:

EngEng: *I wonder (that) he did any work at all!*
USEng: *It's a wonder that he did any work at all!*

EngEng: *I wonder (that) he is not here*
USEng: *I'm surprised that he is not here*

8.   The verb *decide* can be used as a causative verb in EngEng:

Non-causative: *He decided to go because of that*
Causative: *That decided him to go* (i.e., 'caused him to
decide . . .')

In USEng, *decide* cannot be used as a causative; instead, a periphrastic phrase must be used, such as:

Periphrastic causative: *That made him decide to go*

9.   There are a few verbs in EngEng and USEng which differ in the prepositions or prepositional adverbs they collate with:

EngEng	USEng
to battle with/against (the enemy)	*to battle*
to check up on	*to check out*
to fill in (a form)	*to fill out*
to meet (an official = have a meeting)	*to meet with*
to prevent (something becoming . . .)	*to prevent from*
to protest at/against/over (a decision)	*to protest*
to stop (someone doing . . .)	*to stop from*
to talk to	*to talk with/to*
to visit	*to visit with*

10.   In EngEng, the negative form of the first person plural imperative, *let's*, can be either *let's not* or, more informally, *don't let's*. Only *let's not* is used in standard USEng.

11.   In formal styles, the subjunctive is used more often in USEng than in EngEng in *that-* clauses after verbs of ordering, asking, etc. and in conditional clauses. Both varieties can replace the subjunctive in such sentences with *that . . . should* + infinitive or with *to* + infinitive, especially in more informal styles:

USEng—formal	EngEng and USEng—less formal
We recommended that he be released	*We recommended that he should be released*
It is necessary that you do it	*It is necessary* { *that you should do it* / *for you to do it* }
We ask that you inform us as soon as possible	*We ask you to inform us as soon as possible*
If this be the case . . .	*If this* { *should be the case, . . .* / *is the case, . . .* }

12.   Clauses representing hypothetical situations are often introduced by *if*, as in:

If I had been there, I could have fixed it
If you (should) need help, please call me
If this situation were to continue, the authorities would have to take
  action

In EngEng, hypothetical clauses can also be formed without using
if by inverting the subject and verb or first auxiliary:

Had I been there, I could have fixed it
Should you need help, please call me
Were this situation to continue, the authorities would have to take
  action

Such constructions are considered very formal in USEng.
13.   There is a strong tendency in NAmEng to use simple past
tense forms for recently completed events where EngEng would
use the present perfect, e.g.:

NAmEng: *So you finally arrived!*
EngEng: *So you've finally arrived!*

(See also 4.1.3.(6), ScotEng, IrEng.)

4.1.2.   The noun phrase

There are few differences between EngEng and USEng as regards
the noun phrase, and most are non-systematic in nature.

4.1.2.1.   Morphology

1.   As with verbal endings (4.1.1.1.(2)), certain noun endings are
more productive in USEng than in EngEng, e.g.:

-cian: *mortician* ('undertaker'); *beautician* ('hairdresser')
-ee: *retiree, draftee, interviewee*
-ery: *eatery, bootery, winery, hatchery*
-ster: *teamster, gamester*

In general, there is a greater tendency in USEng to use nomi-
nalizations than in EngEng.
2.   For a few words, the derivational ending or the base word that
the ending is put on to is different:

EngEng	*USEng*
candidature	*candidacy*
centenary	*centennial*
cookery (book)	*cook (book)*
racialist, racialism (adjective base)	*racist, racism* (noun base)

sparking plug	*spark plug*
stationers	*stationery shop*
transport (no ending)	*transportation*

3.   Parallel to nouns being used as verbs (4.1.1.1.(2)), verbs can be used as nouns. Again this tends to occur more in USEng than in EngEng, especially with verb-preposition combinations:

Verb	*Noun*
to cook out(-side)	*a cook-out* ('an outdoor barbeque')
to know how (to do something)	*the know-how*
to run (someone) *around*	*the runaround*
to run down (e.g. a list)	*the rundown*
to be shut in	*a shut-in* ('an invalid')
to stop over (somewhere)	*a stop over*
to try (someone) *out*	*a try-out* ('an audition')

4.1.2.2.   Noun class

1.   Collective nouns such as *team, faculty, family, government,* etc. often take plural verb agreement and plural pronoun substitution in EngEng but nearly always take singular agreement and singular pronoun substitution in USEng. While both singular and plural agreement and pronoun substitution with collective nouns are found in both varieties, the choice depends on whether the group referred to by the noun is seen as acting as individuals or as a single unit. There is a tendency in EngEng to stress the individuality of the members, which is reflected in plural verb agreement and pronoun substitution, whereas USEng strongly tends to stress the unitary function of the group, which is reflected in singular verb and pronoun forms. Mixed agreement can also be found in USEng:

EngEng: *Your team are doing well this year, aren't they?*

USEng: *Your team is doing well this year* $\begin{cases} isn't\ it? \\ aren't\ they? \end{cases}$

2.   *Count versus mass nouns.* Count nouns have the following characteristics (among others): they normally occur with an article; that can occur with the indefinite article and cardinal numbers; and they have a plural. Mass nouns, on the other hand, have the opposite characteristics: they can occur with no article; they cannot occur with the indefinite article or cardinal numbers; and they are invariably singular. There are a few nouns which differ in count–mass class membership in the two varieties, e.g.:

(a) *lettuce* has characteristics of both a count and mass noun in EngEng, but it is only a mass noun in many varieties of USEng. It requires a partitive head noun to indicate quantity in USEng:

	EngEng	**USEng** (mass only)
Mass:	*I like lettuce*	*I like lettuce*
Count:	*a lettuce*	*a head of lettuce*
	two lettuces	*two heads of lettuce*

(b) *sport* is a count noun in both varieties but it can also be used as an abstract mass noun in EngEng:

	EngEng	**USEng** (count only)
Count:	*Football is a sport I like*	*Football is a sport I like*
	I like all team sports	*I like all team sports*
Mass:	*John is good at sport*	*John is good at sports*

(c) *accommodation/-s* is an abstract mass noun in both varieties, but instead of being invariably singular as is normal for mass nouns, it is invariably plural in USEng:

EngEng	**USEng**
Good accommodation is hard to find here	*Good accommodations are hard to find here*

3. *Zero plurals.* Some nouns retain the same form for singular and plural (they are said to have a 'zero plural' form), e.g. *sheep*. They differ from invariably singular or plural nouns (like *bread*, *pants*) in that verb agreement does vary from singular to plural even though the noun form does not. There are a few nouns which differ in taking zero plurals in the two varieties, e.g.:

(a) *shrimp* can take a zero plural in USEng but must take a normal plural in EngEng:

EngEng	**USEng**
A shrimp fell on the floor	*A shrimp fell on the floor*
How many shrimps can you eat?	*How many* $\begin{Bmatrix} shrimp \\ shrimps \end{Bmatrix}$ *can you eat?*

(b) *Inning* has the plural form *innings* in USEng. In EngEng, the singular form is *innings* and it has a zero plural:

EngEng	**USEng**
There is one innings left to play	*There is one inning left to play*
There are two innings in a cricket match	*There are two innings in a cricket match*

(c)   When quantitative nouns such as *thousand, million,* etc. are used as modifiers and preceded by a cardinal number, they do not take plural inflection in either variety:

five thousand people
three million dollars

However, when the modified noun is deleted, in EngEng (especially in journalistic EngEng), the plural form of the quantitative noun can be used, while in USEng only the singular can be used:

EngEng only   *The government have cut defence spending*
                       by three millions
USEng (and EngEng) *The government has cut defense spending by*
                       three million

4.1.2.3.   Articles

1.   There are a number of count nouns in both varieties which do not require an article when used in an abstract-generic sense, usually with certain verbs or prepositions: e.g. *in spring, to go by car, to be at church.* However, there are a few such nouns which have this property in one variety but not the other:

EngEng   **USEng**
to be in hospital   *to be in the hospital*

$to\begin{Bmatrix} be\ at \\ go\ to \end{Bmatrix} university$ $to\begin{Bmatrix} be\ at \\ go\ to \end{Bmatrix} a\ university$

$to\begin{Bmatrix} be\ in \\ go\ to \end{Bmatrix} a\ class$ $to\begin{Bmatrix} be\ in \\ go\ to \end{Bmatrix} a\ class$

2.   When referring to events in the past, EngEng does not require the definite article before the phrase *next day.* This construction is more usual in written EngEng:

EngEng   **USEng and EngEng**
Next day, the rains began   *The next day, the rains began*
I saw him next day   *I saw him the next day*

3.   EngEng does not use the definite article in the phrase *in future* in the meaning 'from now on', while USEng does:

EngEng: *In future, I'd like you to pay more attention to detail*
USEng: *In the future, I'd like you to pay more attention . . .*
Both: *In the future, all homes will be heated by solar energy*

4.   In temporal phrases beginning with *all,* the definite article can optionally appear before the noun in EngEng: *all afternoon* and *all*

the afternoon are equally acceptable. In USEng, the construction without the article is by far the more frequent. If the sentence in which the phrase appears is negated, both varieties use the construction without the article: *I haven't seen him all year.*

5. In phrases beginning with *half* followed by some unit of measure, EngEng usually requires an indefinite article before the unit of measure. In USEng, the indefinite article can also come before *half*:

EngEng	*USEng*
half an hour	*a half hour* or *half an hour*
half a dozen (eggs)	*a half dozen* or *half a dozen*
half a pound (of carrots)	*a half pound* or *half a pound*

4.1.2.4. Order of attributes

1. In the written standard, especially in newspapers, EngEng generally places personal attributes after the person named, whereas in USEng the attributes tend to precede the name, often without a definite article:

EngEng	*USEng*
John Smith, the lanky Californian teenage tennis star, won another major tournament today	*Lanky Californian teenage tennis star John Smith won another major tournament today*
Margaret Thatcher, the British Prime Minister, arrived in Washington today	*British Prime Minister Margaret Thatcher arrived in Washington today*

2. For names of rivers, EngEng places the word *river* before the name of the river, while NAmEng uses the opposite order:

EngEng	*NAmEng*
the River Thames	*the Mississippi River*
the River Avon	*the Hudson River*

4.1.2.5. Pronouns

1. The indefinite pronoun *one* occurs in EngEng in formal and educated usage, both spoken and written, while in NAmEng it is usually found only in formal written style. *You* is used instead of *one* in informal styles of both varieties:

Formal: *One has to be careful about saying things like that*
Informal: *You have to be careful about saying things like that*

In EngEng when the indefinite pronoun *one* is used in a sentence, any coreferential pronoun in the sentence must also be *one* (or a form of it), while *he* or *she* (or forms of them) can be used in NAmEng:

EngEng and NAmEng *(formal/educated)*	*NAmEng*

If one tries hard enough, one
    will always succeed
	If one tries hard enough, he/
	    she will always succeed

One must be honest with oneself	*One must be honest with* *himself/herself*

One shouldn't be extravagant
    with one's money
	One shouldn't be extravagant
	    with his/her money

2.   EngEng uses both reciprocal pronouns *each other* and *one another*, while USEng uses mainly *each other*, with *one another* (like *one*) being restricted to formal styles.

3.   Possessive pronouns have two forms in both varieties: a modifier form and a nominal form:

Modifier: *That is their car*
            This is my cat
Nominal: *That car is theirs*
            This cat is mine

In EngEng, the nominal form can be used as a locative when referring to someone's living quarters, while in USEng the modifier form with noun is used in such cases:

EngEng: *Can we come round to yours tonight?*
           We left his about an hour ago
USEng: *Can we come around to your place tonight?*
           We left his house about an hour ago

4.1.3.   Adjectives and adverbs

1.   In some varieties of USEng, a comparative adjective can be used in the phrase *all the ADJ* for emphasis or intensification: *Is that all the better you can do? This is all the bigger they grow.* EngEng does not employ this construction; instead, *any* is used with the comparative adjective (as it is also in USEng): *Can't you do any better (than that)? They don't grow any bigger (than this).*

2.   The adjective *real* is sometimes used as an adverb in informal USEng as in *a real good meal*. EngEng and more formal USEng can only have the adverbial form *really* in such instances: *a really good meal*.

3.   The comparative adjective *different* is usually followed by

from (or sometimes *to*) in EngEng, while in USEng it is more usually followed by *than*:

EngEng: *This one is different from the last one*
This is different from what I had imagined
USEng: *This one is different than the last one*
This is different than what I had imagined

4. One particular adverbial ending is much more productive in USEng than in EngEng: *-wise*. While this ending is used to make nouns into manner adverbials in both varieties, it is also used in USEng to mean 'as far as X is concerned'; as in: *classwise, foodwise, timewise, weatherwise*. This usage is somewhat stigmatized.

5. Adverb placement is somewhat freer in USEng than in EngEng. Those adverbials which can occur medially, before the verb, are placed after the first auxiliary in EngEng if there is one: *They will* never *agree to it. You could* always *have called us first.* In USEng, such adverbs can occur either before or after the auxiliary: *They* never *will agree to it*, or *They will* never *agree to it. You* probably *could have done it yourself*, or *You could* probably *have done it yourself.*

6. The adverbs *yet* and *still* cannot occur with the simple past tense in EngEng, but they can do so in USEng. EngEng uses the present perfect in such cases.

EngEng and USEng *(present perfect)*	**USEng only** *(simple past)*
I haven't bought one yet	*I didn't buy one yet*
Have you read it already?	*Did you read it already?*

7. When the verb *to be* is used in the perfective with the meaning 'to go' or 'to come', the pronominal place adverbs *here* and *there* can be deleted in EngEng and CanEng, but not in USEng:

EngEng and CanEng: *Has the milkman been yet?*
Did you go to the market with them yesterday? No, I'd already been
USEng: *Has the milkman been here yet?*
Did you go to the market with them yesterday? No, I'd already been there

8. The ordinals *first(ly)*, *second(ly)*, etc. are used in both varieties as conjunctive adverbs in the listing of objects, actions, ideas, etc. While both varieties also use the enumerative adverbial phrase *first of all*, only USEng regularly uses *second of all*, *third of all*, etc. in such passages, although this would not be found in formal writing.

9.   The adverb *momentarily* means 'for a moment' in both varieties. However, in USEng it can also mean 'in a moment':

Both:	*He was momentarily stunned*	(for a moment)
USEng only:	*I'll do it momentarily*	(in a moment)

Similarly, the adverb *presently* means 'soon' in both varieties, but in USEng can also mean 'at present' (when the verb is in the present tense):

Both:	*They will be here presently*	(soon)
USEng only:	*They are presently here*	(at present)

10.   Adverbs ending in *-ward* in EngEng denote a purely directional motion while those ending in *-wards* can denote manner of movement also: *backward* ('movement to the back'), *backwards* ('movement back-first'). In USEng *-ward* no longer has a purely directional denotation for most speakers and such adverbs are used interchangeably, e.g.: *frontward(s)*. NAmEng has the forms *toward* and *towards* (identical in meaning). EngEng has only *towards*.

11.   The time adverb *anymore* is used in both varieties in negative contexts, as in *I don't do that anymore* (='I no longer do that?'). In some dialects of NAmEng (particularly Pennsylvania, upstate New York, Ontario and the Mid-West), *anymore* can also be used in positive contexts with the meaning 'nowadays'. Implied in this usage is that whatever is being said to happen nowadays did not use to be the case: the sentence *He comes here a lot anymore* means that he comes here a lot nowadays and did not use to come here a lot. (For a possible origin of this feature, see 5.2.2.)

12.   *Ever* can be used as an intensifier (without meaning 'at some time') in both varieties, but in different contexts. In EngEng it is commonly used with the intensifier *so* before adjectives:

EngEng: *She is ever so nice*
          That match was ever so close

In NAmEng, *ever* can be used informally to intensify verbs in exclamations which have subject–verb inversion:

NAmEng: *Did he ever hit the ball hard!*
          Has she ever grown!
          Am I ever tired!

13.   In CanEng, the adverbial phrase *as well* can occur sentence-initially, whereas in EngEng and USEng it usually appears after the item it modifies:

CanEng: *This has always applied to men. As well,*
it now applies to women
EngEng *This has always applied to men. It now*
and USEng: *applies to women as well*

14. NAmEng has two usages of *over* which are much less common elsewhere. First, *over* can mean 'again', in the sense of repeating an action, usually in connection with the verb *do*:

This is no good—I'll have to do it over
(cf. EngEng: (*all over*) *again*)

Second, it has a locative usage, meaning 'to my place':

We're having a party—why don't you come over

EngEng more commonly uses *round* in this sense.

4.1.4. Prepositions

1. There are a few prepositions which differ in form in the two varieties:

EngEng	*USEng*	
behind	*in back of*	as in *I put it* $\begin{Bmatrix} behind \\ in\ back\ of \end{Bmatrix}$ *the shed*
out of	*out*	as in *He threw it* $\begin{Bmatrix} out\ of \\ out \end{Bmatrix}$ *the window*
round	*around*	as in *She lives just* $\begin{Bmatrix} round \\ around \end{Bmatrix}$ *the corner*

2. Some prepositions which are used identically in most contexts in both EngEng and USEng differ in usage in certain contexts. The majority of such cases occur in expressions of time.

(a) Difference in preposition used:

(i) In phrases indicating duration of time, EngEng uses *for* where NAmEng has a choice of *for* or *in*:

	EngEng and NAmEng	*NAmEng only*
I haven't seen him:	*for weeks*	*in weeks*
	for ages	*in ages*

(ii) EngEng speakers use the preposition *at*, meaning 'time when', with holiday seasons, as in *at the weekend*, *at Christmas* (the season, not the day). USEng speakers generally use *over* in such cases: *over the weekend*, *over Christmas*. EngEng also permits *over* in these cases, and NAmEng also has *on the weekend*.

(iii) In USEng the preposition *through* can mean 'up to and including', as in *Monday through Friday, September 1 through October 15*. In EngEng the 'inclusiveness' must be stated separately if ambiguity is possible: e.g. *Monday to Friday (inclusive)* or *Monday up to and including Friday*.

(iv) In expressing clock-time, EngEng uses the prepositions *to* and *past* the hour while USEng also can use *of*, *till* and *after* (this differs regionally in the USA):

EngEng and USEng	**USEng only**
twenty to three	*twenty of three* or *twenty till three*
five past eight	*five after eight*

(v) *In* and *on* have some differences in non-temporal contexts:

EngEng	**USEng**
to be in a team	*to be on a team*
to live in a street	*to live on a street*
to be in a sale	*to be on sale*
	(Note: *on sale* in EngEng simply means *for sale*.)

(b) Difference in presence of a preposition:

(i) The preposition (usually *on*) is often omitted in USEng before a specific date or day of the week that indicates a time removed from the present:

EngEng	**USEng**
The sale started on Jan. 1st	*The sale started Jan. 1*
(said: 'on January the first')	(said: 'January first')
I'll do it on Sunday	*I'll do it Sunday*

(ii) The preposition can be deleted in USEng before temporal nouns indicating repetition or habitual action (the nouns must become plural if deletion occurs):

EngEng and USEng	**USEng**
He works by day and studies at night	*He works days and studies nights*
On Saturdays we go to London	*Saturdays we go to London*

(iii) In EngEng temporal prepositional phrases, inversion of the noun and the words *this*, *that*, *next* or *last* can occur in formal styles: *on Sunday next, during January last*. Such inversion does not occur in USEng, and the preposition is deleted in the uninverted forms (as in (i) above): *next Sunday*, *last January*.

(iv) In phrases denoting a period of time from or after a given time, the preposition *from* is often deleted in EngEng, but cannot be deleted in USEng:

EngEng	USEng
a week this Tuesday	*a week from this Tuesday*

EngEng also allows inversion in such phrases with no preposition: *Saturday fortnight, Tuesday week.* This does not occur in USEng.

(v) In EngEng, there is a difference in meaning between the phrases *to be home* and *to be at home*:

Is John at home? (Is he physically there?)
Is John home? (Has he returned there?)

USEng can use the second phrase (without the preposition) in the meaning of the first.

(vi) In EngEng, the preposition *from* can be deleted after the verbs *excused* and *dismissed*:

He was excused games at school
He was dismissed the service

This is not possible in USEng.

3.   In interrogative structures involving *how* + certain adjectives, many varieties of USEng employ the preposition *of*:

How big of a house is it?
I wondered how small of a piece you wanted

Such structures are not possible in EngEng.

4.   In sentences such as *The cake has flowers on it, The box with toys in it is mine*, where an inanimate concrete object is designated as having (or not having) a concrete object *in, on, round* or *off* it, the coreferential pronoun *it* can be deleted from the prepositional phrase in EngEng, but not in USEng:

EngEng	USEng
The soup has carrots in	*The soup has carrots in it*
I want some paper with lines on	*I want some paper with lines on it*
This shirt has two buttons off	*This shirt has two buttons off it*
What kind is that tree with flowers round?	*What kind is that tree with flowers around it?*
I'd like toast without butter on	*I'd like toast without butter on it*

4.1.5. Subordinators

1.   The complex subordinators *as . . . as* and *so . . . as* are used with different frequencies in the two varieties. *So . . . as* is fairly infrequent in USEng, being used mainly at the beginning of a clause, while in EngEng it tends to be used more than *as . . . as*:

EngEng	USEng
It's not so far as I thought it was	*It's not as far as I thought it was*
So long as you're happy, we'll stay	*As long as you're happy, we'll stay*
Now we don't go there so much (as we used to)	*Now we don't go there as much (as we used to)*
That one isn't so nice (as the other)	*That one isn't as nice (as the other)*

In cases where *as . . . as* is preferred in EngEng and used at the beginning of a clause, the first *as* may be dropped:

EngEng	USEng
Strange as it may seem, . . .	*As strange as it may seem, . . .*
Much as I would like to go, . . .	*As much as I would like to go, . . .*

2.   In EngEng, the adverbs *immediately* and *directly* can function as subordinators. In USEng, they must modify a subordinator, such as *after*:

EngEng	USEng
Immediately we went, it began to rain	*Immediately after we went, it began to rain*
Go to his office directly you arrive	*Go to his office directly after you arrive*

3.   For many, particularly older, USEng speakers, *why* can function as a subordinator especially in conditional sentences:

If you have any problems, why, just ask for help

4.2. Spelling and punctuation differences

4.2.1. Standard spellings

There are sets of regular spelling differences that exist between the English and American varieties of English. Some are due to American innovations or to overt attempts at spelling regularization (especially by Noah Webster in his 1806 dictionary). Others simply reflect the fact that English spelling was variable in earlier times and the two varieties chose different variants as their standard. Below is a list exemplifying the major spelling differences. No attempt has been made to include every word falling under the particular spelling correspondence; we have indicated if the set is a restricted one. CanEng usage in some cases follow USEng, in others EngEng, and in yet others is variable.

1.	***EngEng: -our***	***USEng: -or***	(but not in words
	colour	*color*	ending in -*or*
	favour	*favor*	signifying persons,
	honour	*honor*	e.g. *emperor*,
	labour	*labor*	*governor* in both
	odour	*odor*	varieties; these
	vapour	*vapor*	spellings are also
			widely used in
			AusEng, especially in
			Victoria)
2.	***EngEng: -ou-***	***USEng: -o-***	(restricted lexical set;
	mould	*mold*	cf. *boulder* in both
	moult	*molt*	varieties)
	smoulder	*smolder*	
3.	***EngEng: -ae/oe-***	***USEng: -e-***	(in Greek
	anaesthetic	*anesthetic*	borrowings; USEng
	encyclopaedia	*encyclopedia*	sometimes uses
	mediaeval	*medieval*	EngEng spelling in
	amoeba	*ameba*	scholarly works)
	foetus	*fetus*	
	manoeuvre	*maneuver*	
4.	***EngEng: en-***	***USEng: in-***	(restricted; cf.
	encase	*incase*	*envelope, incur* in
	enclose	*inclose*	both varieties; *inquire*
	endorse	*indorse*	also used in EngEng;
	enquire	*inquire*	EngEng spelling
	ensure	*insure*	preferred in USEng
	enure	*inure*	in all but last three
			items)
5.	***EngEng: -dgement***	***USEng: -dgment***	(EngEng spelling also
	abridgement	*abridgment*	possible in USEng)
	acknowledgement	*acknowledgment*	
	judgement	*judgment*	

6. | *EngEng: -re* | *USEng: -er* |
    |---|---|
    | *centre* | *center* |
    | *fibre* | *fiber* |
    | *litre* | *liter* |
    | *metre* | *meter* |
    | *spectre* | *specter* |
    | *theatre* | *theater* |

7. | *EngEng: -ce* | *USEng: -se* |
    |---|---|
    | *defence* | *defense* |
    | *licence* (n.) | *license* (n. and v.) |
    | *offence* | *offense* |
    | *practice* (n.) | *practise* or *practice* (n.) |
    | *pretence* | *pretense* |

8. | *EngEng: -ise* | *USEng: -ize* | (USEng spelling is also possible in EngEng; CanEng spelling usually has -*ize* when the stem is transparent— *capitalize*, *glamorize*, *naturalize*—and -*ise* when it is not— *apologise*, *realise*; EngEng and NAmEng both normally have *advertise*) |
    |---|---|---|
    | *apologise* | *apologize* | |
    | *capitalise* | *capitalize* | |
    | *dramatise* | *dramatize* | |
    | *glamorise* | *glamorize* | |
    | *naturalise* | *naturalize* | |
    | *satirise* | *satirize* | |

9. | *EngEng: -xion* | *USEng: -ction* | (USEng spelling also possible in EngEng; restricted, cf. *inspection* and *complexion* in both varieties) |
    |---|---|---|
    | *connexion* | *connection* | |
    | *deflexion* | *deflection* | |
    | *inflexion* | *inflection* | |
    | *retroflexion* | *retroflection* | |

10. | **EngEng: doubled consonant** | **USEng: single consonant** | (only before an ending that starts with a vowel, stress not on last syllable of stem; EngEng spelling also used in USEng) |
    |---|---|---|
    | *counsellor* | *counselor* | |
    | *kidnapper* | *kidnaper* | |
    | *levelled* | *leveled* | |
    | *libellous* | *libelous* | |
    | *quarrelling* | *quarreling* | |
    | *travelled* | *traveled* | |
    | *worshipping* | *worshiping* | |

11.	*EngEng: single -l-*	*USEng: double -l-*	(before an ending
	fulfilment	*fulfillment*	that starts with a
	instalment	*installment*	consonant or at the
	skilful	*skillful*	end of a polysyllabic
	enthral	*enthrall*	word that has stress
	instil	*instill*	on the last syllable)
	fulfil	*fulfill*	

12.	*EngEng: -gg-*	*USEng: -g-*	(restricted to a few
	faggot ('bundle of	*fagot* (but *faggot*	words)
	sticks)	slang,	
		'homosexual')	
	waggon	*wagon*	

13.	*EngEng: -st*	*USEng: no ending*	(restricted to a few
	amidst	*amid*	words; USEng
	amongst	*among*	spelling also possible
	whilst	*while*	in EngEng; spelling
			differences reflected
			in pronunciation)

14. **Miscellaneous**

EngEng	**USEng**	
buses	*busses* or *buses*	
cheque (banking)	*check*	
draught	*draft*	
gaol	*jail*	
gauge	*gage* or *gauge*	
jewellery	*jewelry*	
kerb	*curb*	
moustache	*mustache*	
plough	*plow*	
programme	*program*	
pyjamas	*pajamas* or *pyjamas*	
sorbet	*sherbet*	(different pronunciation)
speciality	*specialty*	
storey (of a building)	*story*	(different pronunciation)
sulphur	*sulfur*	
toffee	*taffy*	
tsar	*czar*	(different pronunciation)
tyre	*tire*	
whisky	*whiskey*	
woollen	*woolen*	

15.	**EngEng:** **hyphenated** **words**	**USEng: fused or** **two separate** **words**	(in compounds and words with stressed prefixes; hyphen is
	ash-tray	*ashtray* (also EngEng)	usually kept in USEng if identical
	book-keeper	*bookkeeper*	vowels are brought
	day-dream	*daydream*	together or if stem
	dry-dock	*dry dock*	begins with capital
	flower-pot	*flower pot*	letter, e.g. *anti-*
	note-paper	*note paper*	*British*, *pre-eminent*)
	anti-aircraft	*antiaircraft*	
	co-operate	*cooperate*	
	neo-classical	*neoclassical*	
	pre-ignition	*preignition*	
	pseudo-intellectual	*pseudointellectual*	
	ultra-modern	*ultramodern*	

16.	**EngEng: retains** **French diacritics**	**USEng: diacritics** **not necessary**
	café	*cafe*
	élite	*elite*
	entrée	*entree*
	fête	*fete*
	fiancée	*fiancee*
	matinée	*matinee*

4.2.2.   'Sensational' spellings

In the USA, and increasingly in Britain, many sensational (and non-standard) spellings which usually involve simplification of the spelling to reflect more closely the pronunciation are used to attract attention, especially in advertising and in tabloid newspapers; they may also be used on roadsigns to save space. The list below gives a sample of common nouns often spelled in a non-standard way; a list of proper nouns (brand names especially) would be exceedingly long.

Sensational	**Standard**
bi	*buy*
donut	*doughnut*
hi	*high*
kool	*cool*
kwik	*quick*
lo	*low*
nite, *tonite*	*night*, *tonight*

pleez	*please*
rite	*right*
sox	*socks*
thanx	*thanks*
tho	*though*
thru, *thruway*	*through*, *throughway*
U	*you*
Xing	*crossing*

4.2.3. Punctuation

There are very few punctuation differences between 'American' and 'English' type of English, and printers and publishers vary in their preference even within the two areas. Typically, however, British usage favours having a lower case letter for the first word of a sentence following a colon, as in:

There is only one problem: the government does not spend sufficient money on education

whereas American usage more often favours a capital letter:

There is only one problem: The government does not spend sufficient money on education

Also, normal British usage is to have a full-stop after a closing quotation mark, as in:

We are often told that 'there is not enough money to go round'.

while American usage has the full-stop (AmEng *period*) before the closing quotation marks:

We are often told that 'there is not enough money to go round.'

Note, however, that if a whole sentence is devoted to a quotation, usage agrees in having the full-stop before the quotation marks:

'There is not enough money to go round.'

4.3. Vocabulary differences

Perhaps the most noticeable differences between EngEng and NAmEng involve vocabulary. There are thousands of words which either differ in total meaning, or in one particular sense or usage, or are totally unknown in the other variety. (There are also a large number of idioms and colloquialisms which differ in the two varieties, but these will not be discussed here.)

Vocabulary differences between the two varieties are due to several factors. The most obvious is that new objects and experiences were encountered in North America which needed naming, either by adapting EngEng vocabulary or by creating new words: e.g. *corn* is the general English term for grain and denotes the most common grain crop, which is wheat in England but maize in North America; the word *robin* denotes a small, red-breasted warbler in England but a large, red-breasted thrush in North America; the words *panhandle* (the narrow part of a state extending outward like a pan's handle) and *butte* (an abrupt isolated hill with a flat top) denote features not found in Britain.

Technological and cultural developments which have occurred since the divergence of two varieties have also been a cause of differences in vocabulary, e.g. terms for parts of cars: US *windshield*, Eng *windscreen*; US *trunk*, Eng *boot*; terminology from different sports: US (from baseball) *home run*, *bunt*, *pitcher*; Eng (from cricket) *pitch*, *wicket*, *bowler*, etc.; differences in institutions of education: US *high school* (14–18 year olds), *major* (=*main subject*), *co-ed* (female student); Eng *public school* (=*private school*), *form* (educational level), *reader* (=*associate professor*), etc.

A third reason for vocabulary differences is the influence of other languages. USEng has borrowed many words (some of which have found their way into EngEng) from a variety of languages, including: American Indian languages—*hickory* (type of tree related to walnut), *hooch* (alcoholic liquor), *moccasin*, *muskie* (type of freshwater fish), *squash*, *toboggan*, and many words for indigenous flora, fauna and geographical features; Spanish—*mesa* (plateau), *tornado* (whirlwind), *tortilla* (thin flat maize bread); African languages—*goober* (peanut), *jazz*, *banjo*; and Yiddish—*schmaltz* (excessive sentimentality), *schlep* (to drag, carry), *schlock* (rubbish).

Finally, independent linguistic change within each variety may be the cause of some differences. One variety may preserve archaisms which the other has lost, or may introduce new meanings for old words which the other has not introduced. CanEng examples of archaisms include *chesterfield* (sofa, couch) and *reeve* (mayor, chief local government officer).

Words used in one variety are often borrowed into the other (unless the thing denoted does not occur in that area). The highest proportion of borrowings is from USEng to EngEng, although examples can be given for borrowings in both directions:

EngEng borrowings from USEng	**USEng borrowings from EngEng**
billion (a thousand million)	*copper (cop)*
brief-case	*penny*
cafeteria	*smog*
teenager	
radio	
snowplow (snowplough)	

In other cases, the differing word might not actually have been borrowed, but it has become known and understood in the other variety: e.g. most EngEng speaker know or will understand that *drapes* are curtains; and most USEng speakers know that a *flat* is an apartment. In still other cases, particularly with slang or idioms, a particular word or sense is not known at all by speakers of the other variety.

We can divide vocabulary differences into four main categories, although there is some overlap.

1. *Same word, different meaning*. This is the category of words which is potentially the most problematic for both foreign and native speakers of one variety, but such examples are few in number. They include:

Word	**EngEng meaning**	**USEng meaning**
homely	'down to earth, domestic' *(=US homey)*	'ugly (of people)'
nervy	'nervous'	'bold, full of nerve, cheeky'
pants	'underpants'	'trousers'
pavement	'footpath, sidewalk'	'road surface'
to tick off	'to scold'	'to make angry'

2. *Same word, additional meaning in one variety*. There are quite a few words of this type, some of which can cause communication problems between speakers of the two varieties. Often the additional meaning is due to a metaphorical extension of the common meaning:

Additional meaning in USEng

Word	**Meaning in common**	**Additional meaning in USEng**
bathroom	'room with bath or shower and sink'	'room with toilet only'
cute	'endearing' (e.g. of kittens)	'attractive, charming' (e.g. of adult people)
dumb	'mute'	'stupid'

good	'fine, nice', etc.	'valid' (as of tickets, special offers)
regular	'consistent, habitual'	'average' (as in size), 'normal'
school	'institution of education at elementary level'	'all institutions of education, including universities'
to ship	'to transport by ship'	'to transport by ship, train, plane or truck'

Additional meaning in EngEng

Word	Meaning in common	Additional meaning in EngEng
frontier	'a wild, open space'	'border between two countries'
leader	'one who commands, guides, directs, is in front'	'an editorial'
to mind	'to heed, obey'	'to look after' (as in *mind your head*, *mind the children*)
rug	'a thick (usually wool) carpet'	'a thick (usually wool) wrap or coverlet' (USEng *afghan*)
smart	'intelligent'	'well-groomed'
surgery	'a medical operation or operating room'	'an office of any doctor'

3.   *Same word, difference in style, connotation, frequency of use.* While words differing in style, connotation, or frequency will usually be understood by speakers of the other variety, it is the use of these types of words which often reveals which variety of English a person has learned. The example words below are marked for differences in style (formal versus informal), connotation (positive versus negative) or frequency (common versus uncommon):

Word	EngEng usage	USEng usage
autumn	common; all styles	uncommon; poetic or formal (*fall* used instead)
clever ('smart, dexterous')	common; positive	less common; usually negative (i.e. 'sly')
to fancy ('to like, want')	common; informal	uncommon

fortnight	common; all styles	uncommon (archaic); poetic
perhaps	all styles	somewhat formal (*maybe* used instead)
quite (as in *quite good*)	negative or neutral	positive
row (/raʊ/; 'quarrel, disturbance')	common	uncommon

4. *Same concept or item, different word.* The majority of lexical differences between the two varieties are of this type. There are two sub-types within this category: that in which the corresponding word is not widely known in the other variety, and that in which the corresponding word is known. Examples of the first type include:

USEng only	*Corresponds to EngEng*
emcee	*compère*
faucet	*tap*
muffler (on car)	*silencer*
rookie	*first year member* (e.g. on a team)
sophomore	*second year student*
washcloth	*face flannel*

EngEng only	*Corresponds to USEng*
dynamo	*generator*
hire purchase	*installment buying*
nought	*zero*
queue	*line*
spanner	*monkey wrench*
treacle	*molasses*

Examples of the second type include:

USEng	*EngEng*
to call (by telephone)	*to ring*
can	*tin*
to check ('to make a check mark')	*to tick*
couch, davenport	*sofa*
game (sports)	*match*
gas	*petrol*
to make a reservation	*to book*
sidewalk	*(paved streetside) path*

Finally, by way of further illustration, we give a brief and arbitrary selection of words that differ in particular semantic spheres. Note that some words, while identical in one semantic sphere or part of speech, can be different in another: e.g. both varieties use the words *hood* and *bonnet* to refer to two distinct types of head covering, but when referring to the covering of a car engine, USEng uses *hood* and EngEng uses *bonnet*. Likewise, while both varieties have the verb *to flex* with identical meaning, the noun *a flex* is used only in EngEng (and is unknown in USEng) to refer to an electric cord.

Food and cooking

USEng	EngEng
cookie (plain)	biscuit (sweet)
biscuit	scone
cracker	biscuit (savoury)
dessert	pudding
pudding	custard
custard	egg custard
jello	jelly
jelly	jam
crepe	pancake
hamburger meat	mince
roast (noun)	joint
eggplant	aubergine
zucchini	courgette
to broil	to grill
stove	cooker
bowl (e.g. for pudding)	basin
pitcher	jug

Clothing and accessories

USEng	EngEng
garter	suspender
suspenders	braces
underpants (women's)	knickers
knickers	knickerbockers
smock	overall
overalls	dungarees
sweater (pullover)	jumper
jumper	dress worn over blouse
undershirt	vest
vest	waistcoat
pantyhose	tights
tuxedo	dinner jacket
barrette	hairslide
changepurse	purse
purse	handbag
diaper	nappy

Household

USEng	EngEng
living room	sitting room
yard	garden
garden	vegetable or flower garden
buffet	sideboard
flashlight	torch
floorlamp	standard lamp
garbage can	dustbin
outlet/socket	power point
sheers	net curtains

Commerce

USEng	EngEng
mortician	undertaker
realtor	estate agent
traveling salesman	commercial traveller
drug store/pharmacy	chemist's shop
hardware store	ironmongers
liquor store	off-licence store
trade (noun)	custom

Transportation

USEng	EngEng
baby buggy	pram (perambulator)
station wagon	estate car
trailer/camper/mobile home	caravan
pullman car (railway)	sleeping car
flatcar (railway)	truck
truck	lorry
pedestrian underpass	subway
subway	underground railway

5
Scottish and Irish English

5.1. Scottish English

English has been spoken in the south-east of Scotland for as long as it has been spoken in England. In the south-west of Scotland it dates from the Middle Ages. In the Highlands and Islands of northern and western Scotland, English has been spoken for only 200 years or so, and indeed Gaelic is still the native language of several tens of thousands of speakers from these areas.

A standardized form of language based on southern Scottish varieties and known as Scots was used at the Scottish court and in literature until the Reformation. Since that time, however, Scots has gradually been replaced in educated usage by Standard English, except in the literature of the likes of Burns and a number of more modern writers (there is currently a strong movement for the revival of Scots). The result is that today educated Scottish people speak and write a form of Standard English which is grammatically and lexically not very different from that used elsewhere, although they speak it with a very obviously Scottish accent. However, the non-standard dialects of southern and eastern Scotland, especially in rural areas, still resemble Scots in many respects and are radically different from most other varieties used in the English-speaking world. In the Highlands, where English was initially learned only in school, forms close to Scottish Standard English are used by all speakers. In this book we concentrate on Scottish Standard English as used and spoken by educated, middle-class urban Scots.

5.1.1. ScotEng pronunciation: vowels

ScotEng pronunciation is very different from that of most other varieties and may be difficult to understand for students who have learned EngEng or NAmEng. Table 5.1 and the recording illustrate a typical ScotEng vowel system:

Table 5.1.   *ScotEng vowels**

/i/	*bee, peer*
/e/	*bay, pair*
/ɛ/	*bed, merry, fern*
/ɪ/	*bid, bird, butter, wanted*
/ʌ/	*putt, hurry, fur, sofa*
/a/	*bad, marry, bard, path, father, calm*
/u/	*put, boot, poor*
/o/	*boat*
/ɔ/	*pot, long, cough, fork, paw*
/ai/	*buy*
/au/	*bout*
/ɔi/	*boy*

* The words in Table 5.1. are also used in the recording for NIrEng (see page 145).

It will be observed at once that there are fewer vowels in this system than in any of the other varieties we have examined. This is due to the following factors:

1.   ScotEng is rhotic. Therefore, the RP vowels /ɪə/, /ɛə/, /ʊə/ and /ɜ:/, which arose in RP as a result of the loss of non-prevocalic /r/, do not occur in ScotEng, and words such as *sawed* and *soared* are distinct. Furthermore, it is a particular characteristic of ScotEng that even short vowels remain distinct before /r/. As a consequence of this, the following pairs are distinguished only by the presence or absence of /r/:

bee	/bi/	*beer*	/bir/
bay	/be/	*bear*	/ber/
fen	/fɛn/	*fern*	/fɛrn/
bid	/bɪd/	*bird*	/bɪrd/
hut	/hʌt/	*hurt*	/hʌrt/
bad	/bad/	*bard*	/bard/
moo	/mu/	*moor*	/mur/
row	/ro/	*roar*	/ror/
pock	/pɔk/	*pork*	/pɔrk/

Note that *fern, bird, hurt* all have *different* vowels; however, they are often merged in middle-class speech.

2.   The RP distinction between /æ/ and /ɑ:/ does not exist in most ScotEng varieties. We write /a/ for the vowel of *bad, bard, calm,* etc. Note that *Pam* and *palm* are therefore homonyms—/pam/. However, some middle-class speakers do have this distinction, probably as a result of the influence of RP.

3.   The RP distinction between /ʊ/ and /u:/ does not exist in most types of ScotEng. *Pool* and *pull* are homonyms—/pul/.

4.   There is no RP-type distinction betwen /ɒ/ and /ɔ:/. We write /ɔ/ for both *cot* and *caught*.

5.   Phonetically, the ScotEng vowels are monophthongs (with the exceptions of /ai/ = [ɛɪ] ~ [ɐɪ]; /au/ = [ɜʉ]; and /ɔi/). Both /ɪ/ = [ɪⱶ ~ ə] and /ʌ/ are central vowels, and /u/ = [ʉ].

6.   All vowels in ScotEng are of approximately the same length, so that /ɛ/ often sounds longer than in EngEng, while /i/ sounds shorter than EngEng /i:/. However, there is a complication in that all the vowels of ScotEng, except /ɪ/ and /ʌ/, are subject to the *Scottish Vowel Length Rule*. This rule has the effect that vowels are longer before /v/, /ð/, /z/, /r/ and word-finally than they are elsewhere. Thus the /i/ in *leave* is longer than the /i/ in *lead*, and the /e/ in *pair* is longer than the /e/ in *pale*. Word-final vowels remain long even if a suffix is added. There is thus a distinction of length in ScotEng between the vowels of pairs such as the following:

Short	**Long**
greed	*agreed*
wade	*weighed*
fraud	*flawed*
toad	*towed*
mood	*mooed*
tide	*tied*
loud	*allowed*

7.   In words such as *serenity*, *obscenity*, the second syllable is often pronounced with /i/, as it is in *serene*, *obscene*, rather than with /ɛ/ as in RP.

5.1.2. ScotEng pronunciation: consonants

1.   ScotEng consistently and naturally preserves a distinction between /ʍ/ and /w/: *which* /ʍɪč/, *witch* /wɪč/.

2.   Initial /p/, /t/, /k/ are often unaspirated in ScotEng.

3.   The consonant /r/ is most usually a flap [ɾ], as in *fern* [fɛɾn] (cf. RP [fɜ:n], USEng [fɜɹn]). Some middle-class speakers, however, use the frictionless continuant [ɹ]. These are usually the same speakers who have merged /ɪ/, /ɜ/, /ʌ/ before /r/ (see above); thus they have *fern* as [fəɹn].

4.   The glottal stop [ʔ] is a frequent realization of non-initial /t/.

5.   /l/ may be dark in all positions; e.g. *lilt* [ɬəɬt].

6.   The velar fricative /x/ occurs in a number of specifically ScotEng words, e.g. *loch* [lɔx] 'lake'; *dreich* [drix] 'dull'. In Scots dialects /x/ occurs in many other words, e.g. *nicht* [nəxt] = *night* (ScotEng [nɛɪt]).

5.1.3. Non-systematic differences between ScotEng and EngEng pronunciation

A few words have distinctively Scottish, or at least non-RP, pronunciations in Scotland:

	ScotEng	**RP**
length	/lɛnθ/	/lɛŋθ/
raspberry	/rasbɛrɪ/	/rɑ:zbrɪ/
realize	/riʌláiz/	/ríəlaiz/
though	/θo/	/ðou/
tortoise	/tɔrtɔiz/	/tɔ:təs/
with	/wɪθ/	/wɪð/

5.1.4 ScotEng grammar

Most of the grammatical differences between ScotEng and EngEng are found at the level of informal speech. They include the following:

1. The full verb *have* behaves more like an auxiliary in ScotEng than in EngEng (see 4.1.1.2.(3)), i.e. in both the present and past tense it can contract and does not require *do*-support for yes–no questions or negation, e.g.:

ScotEng: *He'd a good time last night*
EngEng: *He had a good time last night*

ScotEng: *Had you a good time last night?*
EngEng: *Did you have a good time last night?*

2. As in NAmEng, *will* has replaced *shall* in most contexts. ScotEng goes further than NAmEng in having *will* with first person subjects in questions:

ScotEng: *Will I put out the light?*
others: *Shall/Should I put out the light?*

3. There is a tendency not to contact the negative element *not* in ScotEng, especially in yes–no questions. If an auxiliary is present in a negated sentence, the auxiliary usually contracts.

ScotEng	**EngEng**
Is he not going?	*Isn't he going?*
Did you not see it?	*Didn't you see it?*
He'll not go	*He won't go*
You've not seen it	*You haven't seen it*

4. In sentences like the following, *need* is a full verb with a verbal

complement, as in USEng, rather than a modal, as in EngEng (see 4.1.1.2.(1g)):

ScotEng: *I don't need to do that*
EngEng: *I needn't do that*

Need can occur with a passive participle as its object, as it can in some regional US dialects, whereas most other varieties of English require the passive infinitive or present participle:

ScotEng: *My hair needs washed*
EngEng: *My hair needs washing*
              My hair needs to be washed

5.   *Want* and *need* can have a directional adverb as object as in USEng (see 4.1.1.4.(6)):

He wants/needs out

6.   Certain stative verbs, especially *want* and *need*, can be used in the progressive aspect in ScotEng:

I'm needing a cup of tea

7.   As in USEng, *yes* can occur in ScotEng with non-perfective forms of the verb, while in EngEng it can only occur with the perfective (see 4.1.3.(6)):

ScotEng: *Did you buy one yet?*
EngEng: *Have you bought one yet?*

ScotEng: *He is here yet*
EngEng: *He is still here*

8.   In EngEng the adverbial particle in compound verbs tends to come after the direct object, while in ScotEng it remains directly after the verb, as in many varieties of NAmEng:

ScotEng	***EngEng***
He turned out the light	*He turned the light out*
They took off their coats	*They took their coats off*

All of the above grammatical features are also found in NIrEng.

5.1.5.   ScotEng vocabulary and idioms

The vocabulary of Scots and non-standard Scottish dialects differs very considerably from that of Standard English, to the extent that dictionaries or glossaries may be necessary for reading literature in Scots (e.g. Burns, McDiarmid). ScotEng, on the other hand, differs much less in its vocabulary from other varieties of English.

The differences, nevertheless, are numerous enough. We give a brief list and discussion here of a few of the ScotEng lexical items which may be encountered.

	ScotEng	EngEng
1.	ashet	serving dish
2.	aye	yes
3.	brae	incline, hill
4.	bramble	blackberry
5.	burn	stream
6.	carry-out	take-away
7.	dram	drink
8.	dreich	dull
9.	folk	people
10.	haar	sea mist
11.	infirmary	hospital
12.	to jag	to prick, jab
13.	janitor	caretaker
14.	loch	lake
15.	to mind	to remember
16.	outwith	outside
17.	pinkie	little finger
18.	provost	mayor
19.	rone	drainpipe
20.	rowan	mountain ash
21.	to shoogle	to wobble, shake
22.	to sort	to mend
23.	to stay	to live, reside
24.	through	across
25.	wee	small

Notes

1. *Ashet* is a loan word from French and is unknown in other varieties of English.

2. *Aye* is known by EngEng speakers mainly from archaic sources, songs or nautical usage, but is never used in normal speech in the south of England. In Scotland it is informal but entirely natural.

3. *Brae* occurs frequently in place and street names, and refers to the slope of the hill, not to the entire hill.

4. EngEng speakers talk of *bramble bushes* or even *brambles* for the bushes on which blackberries grow, but ScotEng (and certain varieties in northern England) use *bramble* also for the fruit itself.

5. *Burn* is neutral in style, but is not used in England. Most

EngEng speakers, however, probably know what it means. *Stream* is used in ScotEng in the figurative sense.

6.   Places which sell hot food to be taken away and eaten off the premises are known in Scotland as *carry-outs*. (In the south of England they are *take-aways* and in the north *take-outs*. *Carry-out* and *take-out* are also used in North America).

7.   *Dram* is usually used with reference to whisky.

8.   *Dreich* is a self-consciously Scottish word, i.e. Scots know that English people do not know it, but it is frequently heard.

9.   Both *folk* and *people* are known and used in Scotland and England. *Folk*, however, is much more common and more colloquial in ScotEng: e.g. *They're very nice folk*; *There were a lot of folk there*. In EngEng this type of usage sounds archaic, and *folk* is used mainly as an adjective as in *folk-songs*, *folk-tale*, etc. The ScotEng usage is also found in northern England and in parts of the USA. (Also, the plural *folks* can mean 'parents' or 'family, relatives' in parts of the USA.)

10.   *Haar* is particularly common is the east of Scotland and refers to the thick mist that comes in from the sea.

11.   Scottish hospitals are often known as *infirmaries*, but *hospital* is also common. (Infirmary is also used in the USA, usually referring to a university medical treatment unit where surgery is not performed.)

12.   *Jag* (noun or verb) is frequently used in connection with thorns, injections, etc.

13.   *Janitor* occurs in this usage also in NAmEng.

14.   *Loch*, meaning 'lake', is familiar to most English speakers around the world, from the names of famous Scottish lakes, e.g. Loch Ness and Loch Lomond. The word is originally from Gaelic.

15.   *To mind* has all the meanings is ScotEng that it has in EngEng, but it has the additional meaning, in informal usage especially, of 'to remember' as in *Do you mind when we went to Edinburgh?*

16.   *Outwith* is not known in EngEng but can be frequently encountered in newspapers, public notices, etc. in Scotland.

17.   *Pinkie* is not known by many EngEng speakers, but is widely used in NAmEng also.

18.   The Scottish legal system is separate from that of England and Wales, and many different words are used in legal language, some of them having no counterpart in EngEng. Besides *provost* is ScotEng *procurator fiscal* which corresponds to EngEng *public prosecutor*.

19.   *Rone* in ScotEng can refer to either a downward-drawing pipe outside a house or to the horizontal gutterings around the

roof. EngEng speakers generally have no idea what this word means.

20.   *Rowan* /rɑuən/ is known in England, but there it is normally pronounced /rouən/.

21.   *To shoogle, shoogly* is informal but very usual in ScotEng.

22.   This usage is unknown in EngEng, where *to sort* simply means 'to arrange, to classify'.

23.   *Stay* has all the usual EngEng meanings in ScotEng, but it also means 'to reside, live' as in *I stay at Portobello*.

24.   In discussing east–west or west–east journeys in Scotland itself, speakers often use the word *through*, as in *I'm going through to Glasgow* (from Edinburgh).

25.   *Wee* is known to EngEng speakers but is not often used by them. It is extremely common in ScotEng.

One is also likely to encounter a number of phrases and idioms which are specifically Scottish. A few are listed here:

ScotEng	*EngEng*
How are you keeping?	*How are you?*
I doubt he's not coming	*I expect he's not coming*
Away to your bed	*Go to bed*
That's me away	*I'm going now*
I've got the cold	*I've got a cold*
It's for your Christmas	*It's your Christmas present*
I gave her a row	*I scolded her*
He gave me a fright	*He frightened me*
I'm finished it	*I have finished it/I'm finished*
I'll get you home	*I'll take* (accompany) *you home*
Cheerio just now!	*Cheerio* (goodbye) *for now!*
To go the messages	*To go shopping*
The back of nine o'clock	*Soon after nine o'clock*

5.2.   English in Ireland

Until the 17th century, almost the whole of Ireland was Irish-speaking, with English speakers confined for the most part to a few towns. Native speakers of Irish are now, however, few in number and are confined mainly to rural areas of the south-west, west and north-west, even though Irish is the official language of the Republic and is taught in schools.

The English that was originally spoken in and around Dublin was introduced for the most part from the west and west Midlands of England and still shows signs of this today. English of this sort has spread to cover most of what is today the Republic of Ireland.

The English of the north of Ireland, on the other hand, has its roots in Scotland, particularly the south-west of Scotland, since it was from this region that large numbers of Protestant settlers arrived, from the 17th century onwards. (The two main ethnic groups of Northern Ireland, today labelled 'Catholics' and 'Protestants', are thus to a large extent descendants of the original Irish-speakers and Scots-speaking settlers, respectively.) For a while, Scots-speaking areas of the far north were separated from English-speaking areas of the south by entirely Irish-speaking areas, and at the level of rural dialects there is still a fairly sharp line that can be drawn across Northern Ireland dividing heavily Scots-influenced Ulster-Scots varieties in the far north from other less heavily Scots-influenced Mid-Ulster varieties.

In this chapter we use the label NIrEng to refer to the ScotEng-origin varieties spoken in the north of Ireland, i.e. Ulster-Scots and Mid-Ulster English, and the label SIrEng to refer to the EngEng-origin varieties of the south of Ireland. This distinction is *not* coterminous with the political division of the Republic of Ireland and Northern Ireland: some areas of the Republic, e.g. Donegal, speak NIrEng, while some of the southern areas of Northern Ireland speak SIrEng.

5.2.1.   NIrEng pronunciation

At the level of educated speech, NIrEng pronunciation differs from that of ScotEng mainly in the following respects (many of which can be heard on the recording):

1.   The vowel /e/ of *bay* may be diphthongized to [ei]. Word-finally, however, it is often [ɛ·], and pre-consonantally it may be a diphthong of the type [ɛə] ~ [iə], e.g. *gate* [giət].
2.   /ɒ/ and /ɔ:/ may contrast, but only before /p/, /t/, /k/. Thus, unlike ScotEng, *cot* and *caught* are distinct, but like ScotEng, *awful* and *offal* are homophonous.
3.   /ɑu/ is often rather different from its ScotEng counterpart. In NIrEng the vowel of *house* may range from [œʉ], [ɛʉ], [æʉ] to [ɐə] and even [ɜɨ]. Middle-class NIrEng can have [ɑʉ] or even [ɔʉ].
4.   /r/ is usually not a flap but a frictionless continuant. Words such as *bird*, *card* are pronounced very much as in NAmEng.
5.   In most NIrEng-speaking areas, /l/ is clear [l].
6.   Intervocalic /t/ is not infrequently a voiced flap [d̯], cf. NAmEng.

The intonation of certain types of NIrEng is also very distinctive and resembles that of south-western Scotland. This can be heard on the recording.

English RP exerts a certain influence on the speech of middle-class Northern Irish speakers.

5.2.2.   NIrEng grammar and lexis

Most of the grammatical and lexical features of NIrEng which differentiate it from EngEng are also found in ScotEng and/or SIrEng (see especially 5.1.4. and 5.2.6.). A distinctively NIrEng grammatical feature, however, is the use of *whenever* to refer to a single occasion, as in *Whenever my baby was born, I became depressed* ('When my baby was born . . .'). North-western varieties of NIrEng also have positive *anymore* as in USEng (see 4.1.3.(11)).

Where NIrEng lexis differs from EngEng, it is usually the same as ScotEng or SIrEng. Of the vocabulary items cited in 5.1.5. (ScotEng), the following (at least) are also found in NIrEng: *aye, brae, burn, carry-out, folk, jag, janitor, pinkie, shoogle, wee*. The word *loch* also occurs in NIrEng but is spelt *lough*. Of the vocabulary items listed in 5.2.7. (SIrEng), *bold, cog* and *delph* can also be found in NIrEng. Other lexical items not found in EngEng include:

NIrEng	EngEng
to boke	'to vomit'
to gunder	'to shout'
to hoke	'to poke around, to dig into, to rummage'
to skite	'to slap, to splash'
to wither	'to hesitate'
throughother	'untidy, messy'

These words are also known in parts of Scotland.

In NIrEng, *bring* and *take* can be used differently than in EngEng, e.g.:

NIrEng: *You bring the children to school, and I'll take them home*
EngEng: *You take the children to school, and I'll bring them home*

(This is also true of some varieties of SIrEng and USEng. And in some parts of the west of Scotland, *take* would be used in both clauses of the above sentence, while in some USEng varieties *bring* would be used in both clauses.)

Of the Scottish idioms and phrases listed at the end of 5.1.5., the following (at least) are also used in NIrEng: *I doubt he's not coming, I've got the cold, That's me away, I'll get you home, to go the messages*. Other NIrEng idioms include:

NIrEng	**EngEng**
He gets doing it	*He is allowed to do it*
It would take you to be there early	*You have to be there early*
I'm not at myself	*I'm not feeling very well*
You're well mended	*You're looking better* (after an illness)

5.2.3. SIrEng pronunciation: vowels

The SIrEng vowel system can be presented as follows (Table 5.2) and can be heard on the recording (note that the length distinction typical of RP is also found here, while it is absent from both ScotEng and NIrEng).

Table 5.2.   SIrEng vowels

/ɪ/	[ɪ]	*bid*
/ɛ/	[ɛ]	*bed*
/æ/	[a]	*bad*
/ɒ/	[ɑ]	*pot*
/ʌ/	[ɔ˞]	*putt, nurse*
/ʊ/	[ʊ]	*put*
/iː/	[iː]	*bee, peer, very̱*
/ei/	[eː]	*bay, pair*
/ai/	[ɜɪ]	*buy*
/ɔi/	[ɔɪ]	*boy*
/uː/	[ʉː]	*boot, tour*
/ou/	[oː]	*boat, hoarse*
/au/	[ɜʉ]	*bout*
/ɑː/	[aː]	*path, calm, bard*
/ɔː/	[ɑː]	*paw, talk, port*
/ə/	[ə]	*sof̱a, wanṯed, horses̱*

The RP vowels /ɜː/, /ɪə/, /ɛə/, /ʊə/ do not occur, since SIrEng is rhotic (cf. 5.1.1.(1)). Note the rounded vowel [ɔ˞] for /ʌ/.

The following points represent variable pronunciation differences:

1.   Words such as *path, dance* may often have /æ/ rather than /ɑː/ (see 2.1.2.(4)).
2.   Words such as *hoarse, mourning* may be pronounced with /ɔː/, (the same as *horse, morning*) rather than with /ou/.
3.   Words such as *nurse* may be /nʊrs/ rather than /nʌrs/ = [nɔ˞ɹs].
4.   In some types of Dublin speech, words such as *pair* may be /pʌr/ = [pɔ˞ɹ] rather than /peir/.

5. Words like *book*, *cook*, *rook* may have a /u:/ rather than /ʊ/.
6. *Many*, *any*, etc. may be pronounced /mæni:/ rather than /mɛni:/.
7. Some words which have /ɒ/ in RP may have /ɔ:/ in SIrEng (cf. NAmEng, 3.1.1.(2e)). These words include *dog*, *doll*, *cross*, *lost*, *often*, *wrong*.

At the level of uneducated speech the following pronunciations, which may also appear in the informal speech of educated speakers, can be found:

1. *tea*, *please*, *sea*, etc. with /ei/ rather than /i:/: e.g. *tea* [tʰeː]. This can also be heard in NIrEng.
2. *old*, *cold*, *bold* etc. with /ɑu/ rather than /ou/: e.g. *old* [ɜuld]. This feature is also found in NIrEng.
3. a tendency to neutralize the opposition /ai/–/ɔi/ in favour of /ai/: e.g. *oil* /ail/.

5.2.4. SIrEng pronunciation: consonants

1. SIrEng is rhotic. The /r/ is normally a retroflex approximant, as in NAmEng and NIrEng.
2. The contrast between /ʍ/ and /w/ is preserved: *which* /ʍɪč/, *witch* /wɪč/.
3. /l/ is clear [l] in all positions.
4. Final voiceless plosives /p/, /t/, /k/ are released, aspirated, and without glottalization. In the speech of Dublin, there may also be considerable affrication in final position: e.g. *back* [bakx], *top* [tʰɑpɸ].
5. The influence of Irish phonetics and phonology manifests itself in the treatment of the contrasts /t/-/θ/ and /d/-/ð/. In many varieties the contrast is not preserved, with the dentals /t̪/ and /d̪/ being used throughout. In other varieties the contrast may be preserved in ways other than that employed by RP. For example:

	tin	*thin*
RP	[tʰ]	[θ]
SIrEng	[t̪ʰ]	[tʰ]
or	[t̪ʰ]	[t̪ʰ]
or	[t̪ʰ]	[θ]
or	[θ]	[t̪θ]

(The clusters /tr/ and /dr/ are realized as [t̪ɾ] and [d̪ɾ] by nearly all SIrEng speakers: e.g. *drop* [d̪ɾɑpʰ]. This is true also of speakers of NIrEng.)

5.2.5.   Stress in SIrEng

Distinctively SIrEng stress placement is found in a few words:

SIrEng	*EngEng*
discípline	díscipline
architécture	árchitecture

5.2.6.   SIrEng grammar

There are a number of grammatical differences between SIrEng and EngEng. Most of the typically SIrEng forms are found only in speech, particularly in colloquial styles. They include:

1.   The auxiliary *shall* is relatively rare, as in ScotEng, NIrEng and NAmEng. Instead, *will* is generally used.

2.   Progressive verb forms are more frequent and are subject to fewer restrictions than in other varieties of English. For example, they can occur with many stative verbs:

I'm seeing it very well
This is belonging to me

3.   The simple past tense is used when the sequence of tenses would require the past perfect in other English varieties:

SIrEng: *If he saw her, he would not have done it*
Other Eng: *If he had seen her, he would not have done it*

4.   An aspectual distinction between habitual and non-habitual actions or states is signalled by placing *do*, inflected for tense and person, before the habitual verb:

Habitual	**Non-habitual (on a single occasion)**
I do be drunk	*I am drunk*
(=I am habitually drunk)	(=I am drunk now)
He does be writing	*He is writing*

5.   A calque (loan-translation) from Irish involves the use of the adverb *after* with a progressive where a perfective would be used in other varieties:

SIrEng: *I'm after seeing him*
Other Eng: *I have just seen him*

The perfect is also avoided in other contexts:

SIrEng	*EngEng*
How long are you here?	*How long have you been here?*
Did you have your dinner yet?	*Have you had your dinner yet?*
(cf. NAmEng, ScotEng)	

This feature of perfect-avoidance is also typical of NIrEng.
6.   *Let* can be used with second person imperatives: *let you stay here* (= 'Stay here').
7.   Clefting is frequently used and is extended to use with copular verbs, which is not possible in other varieties:

It was very ill that he looked
Is it stupid you are?

8.   Indirect questions may retain question-inversion and lack a subordinator (*if/whether*):

SIrEng: *I wonder has he come*
Other Eng: *I wonder if he has come?*

This also occurs in NIrEng.
9.   *Yes* and *no* tend to be used less frequently than in other varieties. Instead, ellipted verb phrases are used, as in Irish, e.g.:

Are you going?   *I am*
Is it time?   *It is*
Did he come?   *He did not*

10.   The conjunction *and* can be used to connect simultaneous events in all English varieties, as in *John sang and Mary played the piano*. In SIrEng it can additionally be used to connect a finite clause with a non-finite clause, and is perhaps best 'translated' into other varieties as 'when, as, while':

SIrEng: *It only struck me and you going out of the door*
EngEng: *It only struck me when you were going out of the door*

5.2.7.   SIrEng lexis

SIrEng vocabulary in most cases follows EngEng rather than NAmEng usage. In those respects in which it differs from EngEng, it often resembles ScotEng. In some cases lexical forms not found in other varieties are due to borrowing from Irish, while in other cases they may be due to preservation of archaic forms. Distinctively SIrEng usages include the following:

SIrEng	*EngEng*
bold	'naughty'
to cog	'to cheat'
delph	'crockery'
evening	'afternoon and evening'
foostering	'fuss'
yoke	'gadget, thing'

Note also the distinctively SIrEng directional terms:

back	= westwards, in the West
below	= northwards, in the North
over	= eastwards, in the East
up above	= southwards, in the South

6

West Indian English and English-based creoles

The focus of most of this book is on varieties of Standard English, the kind of English written and spoken by educated English speakers in different parts of the world. However, in order to explain how certain forms of Standard English came to have the characteristics that they do, it is helpful to go into some detail about various forms of English and related languages which do not come into this category. In this chapter we deal not only with West Indian English (WIEng) and other forms of Atlantic Ocean English but also with English pidgins and creoles.

6.1. English-based pidgins

Human beings appear to be biologically programmed to learn languages in infancy and early childhood: children up to the age of 5 or 6 learn their native language or languages rapidly, fluently and perfectly, and without any overt tuition. Adolescents and adults, on the other hand, tend to be rather bad language learners and only in very rare instances manage to learn foreign languages so well that they can speak them exactly like native speakers.

Whenever someone other than a small child, then, attempts to learn another language, certain processes which stem from this imperfect learning ability will almost always occur. In particular, in the speech of such adult language learners, the language in question will be, to different degrees, *simplified* and *mixed*. Simplification is, paradoxically, a rather complex notion, but it can best be understood as involving chiefly *regularization* and *loss of redundancy*. Regularization, obviously, means treating irregular forms as if they were regular, such as when a learner of English said *I buyed* rather than *I bought*. Loss of redundancy often involves the omission of grammatical material which is repeated elsewhere or is not absolutely necessary for conveying the message intended, as when a learner of English says *she like* rather than *she likes*. Here, the grammatical category of third-person singular is conveyed only by the pronoun *she* rather than by the pronoun and the *-s* ending on the verb.

Mixing is a term which refers to the way in which language learners introduce elements from their own language into the language they are attempting to learn. For example, a French-speaking learner of English will almost certainly have a French accent in their English and may also use certain French grammatical constructions and idioms.

Typically, moreover, compared to the language of native-speakers, adult learners' language will also be *reduced*. Because they do not know so much of the language, and because they use it for a more restricted range of purposes, they will control fewer words, fewer grammatical constructions and fewer idiomatic and stylistic devices.

When a language experiences such simplification, mixture and reduction, we can say that it has been subjected to the process of *pidginization*. When language learning takes place over an extended period, in a classroom, pidginization will tend to be slight. In other cases, however, if contact with the foreign language is minimal and short-lived, and the language is learned or 'picked up' without formal tuition, then pidginization may be extreme. In certain rather special social situations, it can happen that an extremely simplified, mixed and reduced form of language of this type comes to be very useful as a means of communication between groups of people who have no native language in common. It may then, over time, develop a fixed form with norms that are shared by large numbers of speakers which can subsequently be passed on to and learned by others. Such a language is referred to as a *pidgin*.

A development of this type occurred in West Africa, where, as a result of early European contact, a regularized, Africanized, reduced form of English, acquired initially from limited contacts with sailors and traders, became useful as a *lingua franca* among different groups of the indigenous population. It then eventually crystalized into the pidgin language that we today call West African Pidgin English. To this day, West African Pidgin English is widely used as a trading language along the coast of Africa from Gambia right round to Cameroon and Equatorial Guinea. Compared to English, this language is mixed—there are elements in its pronunciation, grammar and vocabulary which are due to indigenous African languages; it is simplified or regularized—there are fewer grammatical irregularities than in English; and it is reduced—it would not be adequate for all the uses that a native speaker would want to put a language to, which is, however, of no significance, since it has no native speakers. (Pidgin languages, by definition, do not have native speakers; a pidgin which acquires native speakers is called a *creole*—see below.) It would be a mistake, however, to refer to this language as 'broken English': West African Pidgin English is a language in its own right, with norms and grammatical rules that speakers have to learn in order to speak and understand the language correctly.

Other well-known English-based pidgins are found in the South Pacific: Tok Pisin in Papua New Guinea; Bislama in Vanuatu; and Solomon Islands Pidgin. These three pidgins are closely related, and all are official languages in their respective countries.

An extract from a Papua New Guinea newspaper written in Tok Pisin

Bilong wanem Gavman i mekim olsem? Ating as bilong dispela em Gavman i pret liklik. Sapos Gavman i larim ol plantesin long han bilong ol pipel bai ol plantesin i no inap mekim winmani. Em, as tingting bilong Gavman. Ol i wari tumas long mekim lo samting i save kamapim winmani. Olsem wanem long pipel? Ating yumi mas toktok olsem. Bisnis bilong Gavman em long tingting long pipel. Bisnis bilong Gavman em long tingting long klos, haus na kaikai bilong ol pipel. Olsem na yumi mas senisim pasin bilong ronim ol plantesin. Plantesin i mas sevim ol pipel. I no ol pipel i sevim plantesin.

6.2. English-based creoles

In certain rather exceptional social circumstances, it can happen that a pidgin language acquires an importance over and above its use as a trading language or lingua franca. Indeed, in some cases it can become the most important or even sole language of a community and be passed on to the next generation of children for whom it will be their native language. When a pidgin language takes on a full range of social functions in this way and acquires native speakers, it is known as a *creole*. Like a pidgin, a creole is still, relative to its source language, simplified (regularized) and mixed. It is, however, no longer reduced. Because the language now has to be used for all the purposes a native speaker needs to use a language for, the reduction that took place during pidginization has to be repaired by a process of *expansion*. This expansion process is known technically as *creolization*. During creolization, vocabulary is developed and expanded, grammatical devices and categories are added to, and the language acquires a wide range of styles. Creole languages are thus perfectly normal languages, although their histories are interesting and unusual, and are just as adequate means of communication and expression as any other human language.

There are many English-based creoles in the world, and the number is growing: Tok Pisin, Bislama and Solomon Islands Pidgin are all currently going through the creolization process, as is West African Pidgin English, particularly in Nigeria and Cameroon. Probably a majority of English-based creoles, however, are spoken in the Atlantic Ocean area, where they are a result of the slave-trade. As slaves from many different African ethnic groups were assembled on the coast of West Africa and transported to the Americas, they found, in their multilingual situation, that English-based pidgin varieties were a vital means of communication, and in many parts of the Western Hemisphere, creole languages developed as a result of this need.

One country where a number of English-based creoles are spoken is Surinam, in South America. The two most important of the Surinam creole languages are Djuka and Sranan. Sranan is the native language of a large section of the population of Surinam and is also widely used as a lingua franca by Surinamese people who are not native speakers. Here is a short piece of Sranan which illustrates how far the processes of pidginization and creolization have removed this language from its English source:

> *Den ben sabi f'a b'e weri, fu di a b'e wroko tranga, dan te bakadina a b'e kot wan pis presi opo na libasey.*

'They knew how tired he was, because he had worked hard, then in the afternoon he cleared a piece of ground on the river bank.'

It is obvious that many of the words here are derived from English:

den	'them'
ben	'been'
weri	'weary'
fu	'for'
wroko	'work'
tranga	'strong'
dan	'then'
kot	'cut'
wan	'one'
pis	'piece'
presi	'place'
libasey	'riverside'

However, the phonological and grammatical structures of the language are obviously very different from English—*ben*, for example, is a past tense marker that is placed before a verb stem—and mutual intelligibility with English is certainly not possible. Clearly, Sranan, although historically related to English, is now a separate language.

6.3. Decreolization

There are a number of other English-based creoles, however, which have a closer relationship with English. Surinam was a Dutch colony until 1975, and most speakers of Sranan had little or no contact with the English language—if they did learn a European language, it was Dutch. In many other parts of the world, however, speakers of other English-based creoles have had much more contact than Sranan speakers, during the course of the centuries, with speakers of English itself. Where such contact has been considerable, a process of *decreolization* has normally occurred. What this means is that, because English had higher status than the English-based creoles spoken by the exploited, impoverished, powerless and therefore low-status slaves, the creoles were influenced by English and became less different from it. This process of decreolization involved the creole languages undergoing differing amounts of *complication* and *purification*. Complication reintroduced certain irregularities from English, and counteracted the simplification that had occurred during pidginization. And purification removed certain of the elements from African and other languages that had resulted from the mixing that took place during pidginization.

There are many such English-based creoles that resemble English more closely than Sranan does, because their speakers have had closer contact with speakers of English. In the Pacific area, Hawaiian Creole English comes into this category, as does, in Africa, the Krio language spoken in Sierra Leone by the descendants of freed American, Caribbean and British slaves. Most of the partly decreolized creoles of this type, however, are spoken in and around the Caribbean, notably in Jamaica, Belize, Trinidad and Tobago, and Guyana, as well as on the smaller islands of Anguilla, Antigua, Montserrat, Nevis, Saba, St Eustatius, St Kitts and St Maarten, and in the Cayman Islands and the eastern coastal areas and/or offshore islands of Honduras, Nicaragua, Costa Rica, Panama and Colombia. A similar creole, known as Gullah, is also spoken on islands off the coast of South Carolina and Georgia in the United States.

In those West Indian locations where English is the official language (i.e. not in Saba or St Eustatius, where the official language is Dutch, nor in the Central American countries, where it is Spanish), we frequently find a social continuum of language varieties, stretching from Standard English at the top of the social scale to 'deep' creoles at the bottom. There is, in other words, no sharp linguistic division between Creole and English. This is the situation which is found in Jamaica. Jamaican Creole is probably the best described of the Caribbean creoles, and has the vowel system outlined in Table 6.1.

Table 6.1.   *Jamaican Creole vowels*

/ɪ/	*pit*
/ɛ/	*pet*
/a/	*pat, pot, one, father*
/ʊ/	*put*
/o/	*putt, bird*
/iː/	*bee*
/uː/	*boot*
/aː/	*bard, paw*
/oː/	*board*
/ie/	*bay, peer, pair*
/uo/	*boat, for, port*
/ai/	*buy, boy*
/au/	*bout*

The following features of Jamaican Creole pronunciation can also be noted:

1.   There is no distinction between /a/ and /ɔ/, or between /ai/ and /ɔi/. Note, however, that after some initial consonants some pairs of words are still distinct, for example:

cat	/kjat/	*boil*	/bwail/
cot	/kat/	*bile*	/bail/

2.   Words ending in /aun/ in other forms of English are pronounced with /oŋ/ in Jamaican Creole, e.g. *town* /toŋ/ (the same as *tongue*).

3.   Jamaican Creole is non-rhotic.

4.   The Jamaican Creole consonantal system does not have the distinctions /t/-/θ/ and /d/-/ð/, with /t/ and /d/ being the only phonemes used from each pair: e.g. *thing* /tɪŋ/; *them* /dɛm/.

5.   Consonant clusters are often reduced, both initially and finally, but far more extensively in final position:

scratch	/krač/
strong	/traŋ/
child	/čail/

6. Most forms of Jamaican Creole lack /h/:

house	/aus/
hill	/ɪl/

Like Sranan, although not to the same extent, the grammar of Jamaican Creole is at many points very different from that of English. For example, tense and aspect in verbs are signalled by placing particles before the verb stem:

mi guo	'I go'
mi de guo	'I'm going'
mi bin guo	'I went'
mi bin de guo	'I was going'

The lexis of Jamaican Creole, as a result of the mixing process discussed above, contains a number of words of African origin. Perhaps the best known of these is the word *nyam*, which means 'to eat' and which comes from the West African language Fulani.

6.4. Post-creoles and mesolectal varieties

In places like Jamaica where there is a social dialect continuum, with Standard English at the top, an English-based creole at the bottom, and intermediate varieties in between, it is usual to refer to the most standard 'top' varieties as *acrolects*, the intermediate varieties as *mesolects*, and the 'deepest', most creole-type varieties as *basilects*.

The grammar of mesolectal varieties of Jamaican English demonstrates some creole-like features, many of which result initially from the simplification process which occurred during pidginization. (It is important to stress here that the term *simplification* is a purely technical term, as discussed in 6.1., and is not in any sense value-laden—there is absolutely no suggestion that the language variety in question is in any way inadequate or underdeveloped.)

Grammatical features typical of mesolectal Jamaican varieties include the following:

1. Absence of plurality marking on nouns, if the context or a quantifier makes this clear: e.g. *five book* ('five books').
2. Absence of possessive markers on nouns: *this man brother* ('this man's brother').
3. Absence of 3rd person *-s* on verbs: *He like it* ('He likes it').
4. Absence of the copula in equational sentences and with progressives:

She very nice ('She is very nice')
He going home now ('He is going home now')

5.   Absence of formally marked passives:

That thing use a lot ('That thing is used a lot')

6. Absence of tense markers on verbs; instead, tense may be marked by adverbs or periphrastically with *do*:

$$\left.\begin{array}{l}\textit{He walk home last night} \\ \textit{He did walk home last night}\end{array}\right\}\text{('He walked home last night')}$$

7.   In sentences like *He is easy to annoy*, EngEng interprets the grammatical subject (*he*) of the main verb (*easy*) as the semantic object of the subordinate verb (*annoy*); thus, the sentence can be paraphrased as *It is easy for people to annoy him*. In WI creoles and WIEng the grammatical subject may also be interpreted as the semantic subject of the subordinate verb; thus, a paraphrase could be *It is easy for him to annoy people*, which has a completely different meaning.

8.   In WH-word questions, subject–verb inversion may occur:

What time it is?
Who this is?
Why you are leaving?

There are areas of the West Indies where no 'deep' Creoles are spoken but where the English shows certain mesolectal, creole-type features. In Grenada, the Grenadines, St Vincent, Dominica and St Lucia, we can be rather sure that this is because these islands were originally (and still are to a certain extent) French Creole-speaking and have become English-speaking only relatively recently. The English of Barbados, on the other hand, may represent—although this is not accepted by all experts—a language variety in the final stages of the decreolization process. In other words, it was originally an English-based creole which has over the years become so decreolized that it is now obviously English, but with a few creole features remaining. The English varieties spoken by Black speakers in Bermuda, the Bahamas, and the Turks and Caicos Islands, which also show relatively few creole features, may have a similar origin.

It is also believed by most experts that American *Black Vernacular English* (see 3.3.1.3.), the kind of USEng spoken by lower-class Black Americans and sometimes referred to in the USA as African–American English, has a similar kind of background, i.e. it too may represent a historical English-based creole in the last stages of decreolization. (Related forms of English are also spoken by the descendants of freed American slaves in the West African country of Liberia and in a small area of the Dominican Republic.) Once again, this is clearly a variety of English, but it does share a number of features which are not found in White American dialects with the Caribbean creoles. These features, some of which occur only variably, include the following (compare with (1)–(8) above):

1. Absence of plurality marking on nouns.
2. Absence of possessive markers on nouns.
3. Absence of 3rd person -*s* on verbs.
4. Absence of the copula.

American Black Vernacular English also retains certain traces of the mixing process, preserving, in particular, a number of words of African origin. In fact, some words of African origin have found their way via American Black English into other English varieties. The most famous of these is *OK*, which almost certainly originated in West African languages such as Mandingo.

The West Indies is the one area of the world where the majority of English speakers are of Black African origin. There are, however, a number of communities of people of White European origin. The White population of many parts of the Bahamas speak varieties of English which are basically of a NAmEng type, but with some West Indian features. Indigenous White speakers in Bermuda (not, in fact, part of the West Indies, but with a number of cultural and historical similarities) speak a variety which is also of this type and which resembles most closely the coastal varieties of USEng Lower Southern (see 3.3.1.1.). The White populations of Saba and of the Cayman Islands, however, speak a variety of English which is clearly Caribbean.

6.5. West Indian Standard English

Standard English with distinctive Caribbean characteristics, as we have already noted, is spoken acrolectally in places such as Jamaica, Trinidad and Guyana by speakers towards the top of the social scale. The accents used vary somewhat from place to place. In Jamaica, while the phonetics of the English of educated speakers is very similar to that used by creole speakers, the phonology is rather different and resembles RP much more closely. In acrolectal varieties, for example, /h/ occurs, and the vowels of *bud* and *bird*, *pat* and *pot*, *peer* and *pair*, *buy* and *boy*, etc. are distinguished. Some non-RP features do occur, however:

1.   The /ʌ/ vowel of *but* retains some lip-rounding.
2.   /æ/ is an open [a].
3.   /ei/ and /ou/ are monophthongal [e:] and [o:].
4.   Jamaican English is often rhotic, especially in more formal styles.
5.   /l/ is clear in all positions, as in IrEng.
6.   Final consonant clusters may be reduced:

child	/čail/
tact	/tak/
wind	/wɪn/

7.   A distinctive characteristic of Caribbean creoles lies in their systems of stress, rhythm and intonation. Unstressed /ə/, for example, is much less likely to occur than in most forms of English:

	Jamaican Creole	**EngEng**
Jamaica	[ĭamieka]	[ĭəmeɪkə]
daughter	[da:ta]	[dɔ:tə]
wonderful	[wandaful]	[wʌndəfəɫ]

This trait carries over into Jamaican English (JamEng) and other Caribbean Englishes, and there is a tendency for them to be 'syllable-timed' in their pronunciation, like French, rather than 'stress-timed', like other varieties of English. This means that each syllable occurs at approximately regular intervals rather than, as in other forms of English such as EngEng or USEng, each *stressed* syllable occurring at approximately regular intervals. This can initially make Caribbean English difficult to understand for those unused to it.

Varieties of English in the West Indies have some lexical items which are not found elsewhere; some of them are found throughout the territory, while others are restricted to particular locations.

Colloquial Jamaican English words which are likely to be encountered and may cause particular difficulty include:

JamEng	**EngEng**
to carry (as in *I'll carry you home*)	'to take, transport'
dread	'terrible, excellent'
dunny	'money'
duppy	'ghost'
facety	'cheeky'
foot	'leg and foot'
ganja	'marijuana'
licks	'a beating'

to look for	'to visit'
to mash up	'to destroy, ruin, break-up' (of a marriage)
peelhead	'a bald-headed person'
a something	'a thing'
to stain	'to taste sour, to be sticky'
tall	'long' (of hair)
vex	'annoyed'

Standard Caribbean English is illustrated on the tape with a speaker from Dominica.

6.6. English-based creoloids

A very different creole-like variety of English is spoken in two different locations in the Pacific Ocean area: Pitcairn Island in the remote eastern Pacific and Norfolk Island to the east of Australia. This fascinating form of English is a result of the mutiny among the seamen on the British ship *The Bounty*, after which nine British mutineers escaped, in 1790, to hide on Pitcairn, which was uninhabited at the time, together with six Tahitian men and twelve Tahitian women. The language developed by their descendants, which is often referred to as Pitcairnese, shows a number of features due to simplification, together with very considerable mixture, particularly in vocabulary, from Tahitian, a Polynesian language. In 1856 a large number of people from Pitcairn were relocated on Norfolk Island, where their descendants are now outnumbered by more recent settlers from Australia and elsewhere. Those there who are still able to speak Pitcairnese, or 'Norfolk' as it is often referred to on the island, are all also bilingual in English.

Mixed and somewhat simplified varieties of English are also spoken in two different locations in the South Atlantic. The island of St Helena has a population of about 6000, of mixed European, African and Asian origin. The very remote island of Tristan da Cunha has a population of about 300, of mainly British but also partly American, Dutch and Italian origin.

Pitcairnese, St Helena English and Tristan English resemble the post-creoles of the West Indian area in that they demonstrate a certain amount of simplification and mixture. Although this is clearly the result of the fact that they have undergone some pidginization, none of these varieties is descended via a creole from a pidgin. They were never subjected to reduction (see 6.1.) and therefore never experienced expansion or creolization. We cannot therefore call them creoles or post-creoles. They are referred to instead as *creoloids*. A creoloid, we can say, is a language variety which has been subject to a certain amount of simplification and mixture, but where a continuous native-speaker tradition has been maintained throughout.

7
Second language varieties of English

English is a language which has more non-native speakers than native speakers. The non-native speakers can be divided into two types. First, there are speakers of English as a Foreign Language who learn English as a vehicle of international communication. People in Germany or Japan or Brazil or Morocco who have learnt English will normally expect to use it in interaction with people from countries other than their own. Second, there are speakers of English as a Second Language. These are to be found in those nations where English is used as an official language, and/or as a language of education, and/or as a means of wider communication within the country, by people who are not native speakers. There are many such countries in the world.

In the Americas, English is an important second language in Puerto Rico, and also has some second-language presence in Panama. In Europe, in addition to the United Kingdom and the Republic of Ireland where English is spoken natively, English has official status in Gibraltar and Malta and is also widely spoken as a second language in Cyprus. In Africa, there are large communities of native speakers of English in Liberia, South Africa, Zimbabwe and Kenya, but there are even larger communities in these countries of second-language speakers. Elsewhere in Africa, English has official status, and is therefore widely used as a second language lingua franca in Gambia, Sierra Leone, Ghana, Nigeria, Cameroon, Namibia, Botswana, Lesotho, Swaziland, Zambia, Malawi and Uganda. It is also extremely widely used in education and for governmental purposes in Tanzania and Kenya.

In the Indian Ocean, Asian, and Pacific Ocean areas, English is an official language in Mauritius, the Seychelles, Pakistan, India, Singapore, Brunei, Hong Kong, the Philippines, Papua New Guinea, the Solomon Islands, Vanuatu, Fiji, Tonga, Western Samoa, American Samoa, the Cook Islands, Tuvalu, Kiribati,

Guam and elsewhere in American administered Micronesia. It is also very widely used as a second language in Malaysia, Bangladesh, Sri Lanka, the Maldives, Nepal and Nauru. (In India and Sri Lanka, there are also Eurasian native speakers of English.)

In many of these areas, English has become or is becoming *indigenized*. This means that these second language varieties of English, as a result of widespread and frequent use, have acquired or are acquiring relatively consistent, fixed local norms of usage which are adhered to by all speakers. These varieties of English may differ, often considerably, from the English of native speakers elsewhere in the world, mainly as a result of influence from local languages. Thus native speakers of English may sometimes have some difficulty in understanding these non-native varieties. This is something of a problem, but it is not clear what should be done about it. If, for example, certain features of West African English (WAfEng) make that variety easier and better than EngEng for West Africans to learn and use, then does it matter that British people find WAfEng difficult to understand? After all, Americans may find ScotEng difficult to understand, but no one would seriously suggest that this is a reason for changing ScotEng. There is, of course, a certain lack of parallel between the ScotEng and the WAfEng cases: (a) the Scots are native speakers; and (b) some West Africans and Indians *believe* that they are speaking EngEng, or at least aim at speaking EngEng.

A particular problem arises in the case of speakers of non-native varieties of English who attempt to get English Language degrees at continental European universities. For example, a West African student's English may be more fluent than that of a Dutch student, but is the WAfEng variety valid or appropriate in the Dutch situation, and, more importantly, should such a student be allowed to teach English in a Dutch school?

There are no easy solutions to such problems. We believe, however, that as long as the differences from EngEng in, for example, an African's or Indian's English do not impair intelligibility greatly, then there is no reason at all to object to that variety being used in native English-speaking areas. Obviously, within Africa or India themselves, the margin for tolerance of differences can be much greater. Equally as important, we believe that native English speakers travelling to areas such as Africa or India should make the effort to improve their comprehension of the non-native variety of English (much as Americans would have to improve their comprehension of ScotEng when travelling in Scotland) rather than argue for a more English-type English in these areas.

We now describe some of these well-established second language varieties of English.

7.1. West African English

WAfEng is spoken by non-native speakers of English in Gambia, Sierra Leone, Liberia, Ghana, Nigeria and Cameroon.

7.1.1. WAfEng pronunciation

The vowel system of WAfEng is typically reduced in comparison to that of most native varieties of English, lacking several vowel contrasts. One type of WAfEng vowel system is given in Table 7.1. Different speakers show different degrees of approximation between this system and that of RP.

Table 7.1. WAfEng vowels

/i/	*bid, bee*
/e/	*bay*
/ɛ/	*bed, bird*
/a/	*bad, bard, <u>fa</u>ther, butt<u>er</u>*
/ɔ/	*pot, putt, p<u>aw</u>, port*
/o/	*boat*
/u/	*boot, put*
/ai/	*buy*
/ɔi/	*boy*
/au/	*bout*

The following features of WAfEng can be noted:

1. WAfEng is non-rhotic. Thus *ten* and *turn* are homophonous.
2. RP /ɪə/ and /ɛə/ correspond to /ia/ and /ea/ in WAfEng:

peer /pia/
pair /pea/

3. Words such as *button, apple* do not have final syllabic consonants as in other varieties of English:

	WAfEng	**RP**
button	/bɔtin/	/bʌtn̩/
apple	/apul/	/æpl̩/

4. Words ending in *mb—bomb, climb, plumb*, etc.—may be pronounced with a final /b/. Similarly, words ending in *ng—ring, long, bang*, etc.—may be pronounced with a final /ŋg/.
5. There is a tendency for final consonant clusters to be reduced: *last* /las/, *passed* /pas/.
6. There is a tendency for final voiced consonants to be devoiced: *proud* /praut/, *robe* /rop/.

7.   A number of words have stress differences from EngEng:

congratuláte
investigáte
madám
mainténance
recogníze
súccess

8.   Contrastive stress is rare. For example, rather than an exchange like:

Did John go to the store?
No, <u>Bill</u> went

one is more likely to find a clefted version for emphasis/focusing:

No, it was Bill who went

9.   WAfEng is typically syllable-timed rather than stress-timed (see 6.5.(7)). This is perhaps the main cause of intelligibility difficulties for native speakers. (Intelligibility difficulties work, of course, in both directions.)

7.1.2.   WAfEng grammar

WAfEng varies quite considerably from place to place: some of the forms we list below, for instance, occur in Ghana but not in Nigeria, or *vice versa*. It also varies very much according to the education of the speaker and the formality of the situation. Some of the forms given here are not, therefore, employed by the most educated speakers, or at least not in writing. Where the grammar of WAfEng differs from that of other varieties of English, this is often (but not always) due to influence from indigenous languages. This influence is most marked in less educated and more informal styles.

Typical WAfEng grammatical forms include the following:

1.   Omission of articles:

I am going to cinema

2.   Pluralization of non-count nouns:

I lost all my furnitures
The damages caused are great

3.   The use of resumptive pronouns, not only after focused nouns, as in some colloquial styles of English:

My brother, he's crazy

but also in relative clauses in a non-English manner:

The guests whom I invited them have arrived

4. No distinction between the reflexive pronoun *themselves* and the reciprocal pronoun *each other*:

The like themselves = 'They like each other'

5. Formation of comparative clauses without using the comparative form of the adjective when it involves *more*:

It is the youths who are skilful in performing tasks than the adults

6. Absence of infinitival *to* after some verbs:

They enabled him do it

7. The use of progressive aspect with *have* when expressing a temporary state:

I am having a cold

8. The use of a universal tag question—*is it?*—regardless of person, tense or main clause auxiliary:

We should leave now, is it? (EngEng: *'shouldn't we?'*)
She has gone home, is it?　(EngEng: *'hasn't she?'*)

9. A non-English use of *yes* and *no* in answering questions:

Hasn't he come home yet?
(a)　*Yes* = 'He *hasn't* come home yet'
(b)　*No* = 'He *has* come home'

cf. also:

It may not rain tomorrow
I hope so = 'I hope it will *not* rain'

7.1.3.　WAfEng lexis

Many differences in vocabulary between WAfEng and other varieties of English involve extensions or alterations to the semantic or grammatical function of English words. Others reflect usages of equivalent words from indigenous languages, while still others are innovations. The list below gives a few examples by way of illustration. Not all the items are found in all West African countries.

WAfEng	*EngEng*
again	'anymore'
amount	besides EngEng meaning, it can also mean 'money'

balance	'change' (i.e. money returned to a customer)
a been-to	'someone who has "been to" Europe or North America' (slightly derogatory)
to bluff	besides EngEng meaning, it can also mean 'to dress fashionably' or 'to show off'
carpet	'linoleum'
corner	'a bend in the road'
chop bar/canteen	'a restaurant serving indigenous food'
coal pot	'a form of brazier for cooking on'
guy	'an outgoing, self-assured young man'
to hear	besides EngEng meaning, one can also 'hear', i.e. 'understand', a language
hot drink	'alcoholic spirits, liquor'
rice water	'rice porridge'
serviceable	besides EngEng meaning, it can also mean 'willing to serve'
sorry	an expression of sympathy to someone who has just had a mishap (corresponds to similar terms in WAf languages); not very usual as an apology
the steer/steering	'the steering wheel of a vehicle'
to take in	besides EngEng meaning, it can also mean 'to become pregnant'

A very distinctive characteristic of WAfEng vocabulary and grammar is the use of 'high' literary style, i.e. the use of long or Latinate words (*epistle* instead of *letter*, *purchase* instead of *buy*) and complicated grammatical constructions not only in writing but also in speech. This could be due to several things, including exposure to literary rather than colloquial English and the prestige of the written word.

7.2.   East African English

English of a distinctively East African type (EAfEng) is spoken as a second language in Kenya, Tanzania and Uganda. The English spoken by Africans in Malawi, Zambia, Zimbabwe and South Africa is also of a very similar type. Most of the indigenous languages in most of these areas of eastern and southern Africa are members of the Bantu language family, and these have naturally played an important role in influencing the nature of EAfEng.

There are many similarities between EAfEng and WAfEng. Differences include the following:

7.2.1. EAfEng pronunciation

1. There tend to be fewer vowels in EAfEng than in WAfEng (8 as opposed to 10; cf. about 20 in EngEng RP), and the way in which sets of words which are distinct in native forms of English are grouped together differs from that in WAfEng. The vowel system of EAfEng is illustrated in Table 7.2.

Table 7.2. EAfEng vowels

/i/	bid, bee
/e/	bed, bay
/a/	bad, bard, bird, putt, father
/o/	pot, boat, paw, port
/u/	put, boot
/ai/	buy
/oi/	boy
/au/	bout

2. Many speakers do not distinguish /l/ and /r/.
3. /č/ and /š/ may be merged with /s/, and /ǰ/ and /ž/ with /z/.

7.2.2. EAfEng lexis

A number of words from indigenous languages are used by EAfEng speakers even when speaking and writing English. These include the following:

EAfEng	*EngEng*
askari	'policeman'
chai	'tea'
duka	'shop'
kibanda	'black market'
manamba	'labourer'
matatu	'taxi bus'
wananchi	'fellow citizens'

7.3. Indian English

In the South Asian sub-continent, English is widely spoken and written in India, Pakistan, Bangladesh and Sri Lanka. We concentrate here on India, where English is an official language and is used as one of the languages of education and wider communication. There are a number of native speakers of English in India, but these are far outnumbered by those for whom it is an additional language.

Like AfEng, Indian English (IndEng) is beset by the problem of norms. There is no general agreement as to whether the standard should be strictly EngEng or whether IndEng forms (especially in grammar) which are used by the majority of educated speakers and can also be found in newspapers should be accepted in the Indian standard.

7.3.1. IndEng pronunciation

The pronunciation of IndEng varies quite considerably depending on the speaker's native language as well as on his or her educational background and degree of exposure to native English. There are, nevertheless, a number of generalizations which can be made.

1.   IndEng tends to have a reduced vowel system *vis à vis* RP (cf. WAfEng above), with some contrasts lacking. Which contrasts these are will depend on the system of the particular native language, but often RP /ɑ:/ and /ɔ:/ both correspond to IndEng /ɑ:/, RP /ɒ/ and /æ/ to IndEng /a/.

2.   The RP diphthongs /ei/ and /ou/ tend to be monophthongal /e:/ and /o:/.

3.   In southern India, word-initial front vowels tend to receive a preceding /j/ and back vowels a preceding /w/: *eight* /je:t/: *own* /wo:n/.

4.   In northern India, word-initial /sk/, /st/ or /sp/ tend to receive a preceding /i/: *speak* /ispi:k/.

5.   The English of most educated Indians is non-rhotic.

6.   /r/ tends to be a flap [ɾ] or even a retroflex flap [ɽ].

7.   In some varieties, /v/ and /w/ are not distinguished; similarly /p/ and /f/; /t/ and /θ/; /d/ and /ð/; /s/ and /š/—depending on the region.

8.   The consonants /p/, /t/, /k/ tend to be unaspirated.

9.   The alveolar consonants /t/, /d/, /s/, /l/, /z/ tend to be replaced by retroflex consonants /ʈ/, /ɖ/, /ṣ/, /ḷ/, /ẓ/.

10.   IndEng differs considerably from other forms of English in stress, rhythm and intonation (as do WAfEng and WIEng). These differences make for difficulties, sometimes very serious indeed, in comprehension on the part of speakers of other English varieties. In particular, IndEng tends to be syllable-timed rather than stress-timed (see 6.5.(7)). Also, syllables that would be unstressed in other varieties of English receive some stress in IndEng and thus do not have reduced vowels. Suffixes tend to be stressed, and function words which are weak in other varieties of English (*of* /əv/, *to* /tə/, etc.) tend not to be reduced in IndEng.

7.3.2. IndEng morphology and grammar

The following morphological and grammatical features are among those that occur sometimes in the English of even some educated Indians and in English-language newspapers in India:

1. Differences in count noun–mass noun distinctions:

(a) the pluralization of many EngEng mass nouns (especially abstract nouns), e.g.:

aircrafts:	*Many aircrafts have crashed there*
fruits:	*We ate just fruits for lunch*
litters (rubbish):	*Do not throw litters on the street*
furnitures:	*He bought many furnitures*
woods:	*He gathered all the woods*

(b) the use of nouns alone which appear only in partitive phrases in EngEng, e.g.:

alphabets:	*He knows many alphabets already*
	(= letters of the alphabet)
a chalk:	*Everyone pick up a chalk*
	(= piece of chalk)
clothes:	*I have bought two clothes today*
	(= items of clothing)
toasts:	*I'd like two toasts, please*
	(= pieces/slices of toast)

2. An extended use of compound formation. In EngEng, noun + noun compounds such as *facecloth*, *teacup* can be made from the construction $noun_1 + for + noun_2$, becoming $noun_2 + noun_1$ (e.g. *cup for tea* becomes *teacup*). IndEng has extended this process to include constructions with other prepositions, notably *of*. Some compounds formed from such phrases are transparent in meaning:

chalk-piece:	'piece of chalk'
key-bunch:	'bunch of keys'
meeting notice	'notice of a meeting'

while others are ambiguous (where *of* can mean 'containing')

fish tin:	'tin containing fish'
	(EngEng 'tin for fish')
water bottle:	'bottle containing water'
	(EngEng 'bottle for water')

Other IndEng compounds consisting of nouns and deverbal nouns include:

age barred	'barred by age'
pindrop silence	'silent enough to hear a pin drop'
schoolgoer	'one who goes to school'

3. The use of nominal rather than participial forms of some words when used as adjectives, e.g.:

colour pencils   (EngEng = *coloured*)
schedule flight   (EngEng = *scheduled*)

4. A difference in use of prepositions in verb–preposition collocations:

(a) no preposition:

IndEng	*EngEng*
to dispense ('do without')	*to dispense with*
to strike ('delete')	*to strike out*

(b) addition of preposition:

to accompany with
to air out (one's views)
to combat against
to fear of
to return back

(c) different preposition:

IndEng	*EngEng*
to be baffled with	*to be baffled by*
to get down (from a vehicle)	*to get off/out*
to pay attention on	*to pay attention to*
to tear off/away	*to tear up*

5. The use of *itself* and *only* to emphasize time or place where EngEng speakers would usually use intonation to provide emphasis:

Can I meet with you tomorrow itself?
We will be required to have our classes here itself
Now only I have understood the problem (= just now)
We arrived today only

6. The use of adverbial *there* for 'dummy' *there*. 'Dummy' *there* in EngEng occurs in subject position with an existential meaning and has reduced pronunciation, while adverbial *there* is not reduced: observe the difference in the two *there*s in *There's* (dummy) *some paper over there* (adverb). In IndEng, one can hear sentences such as the following:

IndEng: *What do you want to eat? Meat is there, vegetables are there, bread is there*
EngEng: *There is meat, there are vegetables, there is bread*

IndEng: *I'm sure an explanation is there*
EngEng: *I'm sure there is an explanation*

7. Different use of some auxiliaries. The auxiliaries *could* and *would* are often used instead of their present forms *can* and *will* because IndEng speakers feel the past forms are more tentative and thus more polite:

We hope that you could join us
Let's finish now so that we could be there early
The lecture would begin at 2:00
We hope that the Vice-Chancellor would investigate this matter

Also, *could* is used in IndEng where EngEng speakers would use *was able to*:

He could just only finish it before we left
I could do well because I studied diligently

The auxiliary *may* is used to express obligations politely in IndEng:

IndEng: *This furniture may be removed tomorrow*
EngEng: *This furniture is to be removed tomorrow*

IndEng: *These mistakes may please be corrected*
EngEng: *These mistakes should be corrected*

8. There are several differences from EngEng in the usage of tense and aspect in IndEng. They include the following:

(a) the use of the present tense with durational phrases (indicating a period from past to present) where EngEng would require the present perfect (unusual in more educated IndEng):

IndEng: *I am here since two o'clock*
EngEng: *I have been here since two o'clock*

IndEng: *I am reading this book since (for) two hours*
EngEng: *I have been reading this book for two hours*

(b) the use of future forms in temporal and conditional clauses where EngEng would require present tense forms:

IndEng: *When you will arrive, please visit me*
EngEng: *When you arrive, please visit me*

IndEng: *If I will come, I will see you*
EngEng: *If I come, I will see you*

(c)   absence of sequence-of-tense constraints

IndEng: *When I saw him last week, he told me that he is*
          coming
EngEng: *When I saw him last week, he told me that he was*
          coming

(d)   the use of progressive aspect with habitual action:

IndEng: *I am doing it often*
EngEng: *I do it often*

with completed action:

IndEng: *Where are you coming from?*
EngEng: *Where have you come from?*

and with stative verbs:

IndEng: *Are you wanting anything?*
EngEng: *Do you want anything?*

IndEng: *She was having many sarees*
EngEng: *She had many sarees*

(e)   the use of the perfective aspect instead of the simple past
(especially with past-time adverbs):

I have been there ten years ago
We have already finished it last week
Yesterday's lecture has lasted three hours
What had you told them on Friday?
I had given it to you yesterday
We had already informed you of that

9.   The absence of subject–verb inversion in direct questions, and
the use of such inversion in indirect questions (which is exactly the
opposite of EngEng usage):

(a)   direct questions with no subject–verb inversion

IndEng: *What this is made from?*
EngEng: *What is this made from?*

IndEng: *Who you have come to see?*
EngEng: *Who have you come to see?*

IndEng: *He didn't go yesterday?*
EngEng: *Didn't he go yesterday?*

(b)   indirect questions with inversion

IndEng: *I asked him where does he work*
EngEng: *I asked him where he works*

IndEng: *I wonder where is he*
EngEng: *I wonder where he is*

10.   The use of a universal, undifferentiated tag question—*isn't
it?*—regardless of person tense, or main clause auxiliary (see
7.1.2.(8)):

You are going home soon, isn't it?
They said they will be here, isn't it?
We could finish this tomrrow, isn't it?

11.   Differences in complement structures with certain verbs,
e.g.:

IndEng: *We are involved to collect poems*
EngEng: *We are involved in collecting poems*

IndEng: *She was prevented to go*
EngEng: *She was prevented from going*

IndEng: *I would like that you come*
EngEng: *I would like you to come*

IndEng: *They want that you should leave*
EngEng: *They want you to leave*

12.   A non-English use of *yes* and *no*, as in WAfEng (see
7.1.2.(9)).

7.3.3.   IndEng lexis

One distinctive characteristic of IndEng is that there is substantial
lexical borrowing from Indian languages into English. Some
frequently encountered words include the following:

IndEng	*EngEng*
bandh	'a total strike in an area'
crore	'ten million'
dhobi	'washerman' (also found in the English of Singapore and Malaysia)
durzi	'tailor'
to gherao	'to demonstrate against someone by not allowing the person to leave his desk/office'
hartal	'a strike used as a political gesture'
lakh	'one hundred thousand'
lathi	'long heavy stick made of bamboo and bound with iron' (used by the police)
sahib	'sir, master'
swadeshi	'indigenous, native, home-grown'

Other vocabulary differences between EngEng and IndEng are due to extension or alteration of meaning of EngEng words, retention of archaic forms or innovations. A brief sample follows:

IndEng	*EngEng*
almirah	'a chest of drawers' (from Portuguese)
appreciable	'appreciated'
as such	'consequently, therefore'
backside	'behind, in back of'
biodata	'curriculum vitae'
co-brother	'wife's sister's husband'
colony	'residential area'
cousin-sister	'female cousin'
eve-teasing	'teasing girls'
furlong	'$\frac{1}{8}$ of a mile' (archaic in EngEng except in horse-racing)
to half-fry	'to fry (an egg) on one side'
hotel	'restaurant, cafe' (not necessarily with lodgings)
jawan	'soldier'
to be out of station	'to be away from the place where one works'
playback artiste	'professional singer who sings offstage while a performer on stage mimes the words'
police firing	'shooting by police'
ryot	'farmer'
stepney	'a spare wheel; a substitute'
stir	'a demonstration; agitation'
tiffin	'lunch'

7.4.   Singaporean English

Singapore is an island nation with a population of nearly 3 million. It was a British colony until 1959. The official languages are English, Malay, Tamil and Mandarin Chinese. Mandarin and English have very few native speakers in Singapore, the majority of the population being native speakers of Hokkien and other varieties of Chinese. The English of Singapore (SingEng), which has many similarities with that of Malaya and other areas of Malayasia, is widely used as a lingua franca within the multilingual society of Singapore, and, not surprisingly, demonstrates a certain amount of influence from Chinese. The type of English described here is that of the most educated segment of the population.

Table 7.3. *The vowels of SingEng*

/i/	bid
/e/	bed
/ɛ/	bad
/a/	putt
/ɔ/	pot
/u/	put
/ə/	sof<u>a</u>
/i:/	be<u>e</u>
/e:/	bay
/ɛ:/	pair
/a:/	bard, father
/ɔ:/	paw, port
/o:/	boat
/u:/	boot
/ə:/	bird
/ai/	buy
/oi/	boy
/au/	bout
/jə/	peer
/wə/	poor

Less standard speakers have many fewer vowels than this and may merge /i/ and /i:/, /e/ and /ɛ/, /a/ and /a:/, /ɔ/ and /ɔ:/, /u/ and /u:/, /ə/ and /ə:/.

7.4.1. The pronunciation of SingEng

The vowel system of SingEng is shown in Table 7.3. Educated SingEng is non-rhotic and has most of the vowel contrasts found in RP. The phonetics of the vowels, however, is rather different. Other pronunciation features include the following:

1. Although SingEng is non-rhotic, it generally lacks linking and intrusive /r/ (see 2.1.3.(4)).
2. SingEng is syllable-timed (see 6.5.(7)).
3. Word-final clusters of three or more consonants are often simplified to two, e.g. *next* /neks/, *punched* /panč/. This has grammatical consequences, in that present tense -*s*, past tense -*ed* and plural -*s* may be omitted.
4. Most usually, /əl/ and /ən/ occur rather than syllabic /l/ and /n/ in words like *bottle, button*.
5. Word-final consonants are usually voiceless, so that /b/, /d/, /g/, /ǰ/, /v/, /ð/, /z/ are merged with /p/, /t/, /k/, /č/, /f/, /θ/, /s/, e.g. *knees = niece, leaf = leave*.
6. Word-final stops are usually glottalized and unreleased: e.g. *rope, robe* [ro:pʔ]; *bat, bad* [bɛtʔ]; *pick, pig* [pikʔ]. For some

speakers, all word-final consonants can be realized simply as [ʔ]: *pick*, *pig* [piʔ].

7.   /θ/ and /ð/ are often merged with /t/ and /d/, respectively.

8.   Post-vocalic /l/ is often vocalized to [ʊ] or lost altogether:

> *milk*   [miʊk]
> *well*   [weʊ]
> *tall*   [tɔː]

7.4.2.   SingEng grammar

1.   As in a number of other forms of non-native English, some mass nouns are treated as count nouns: *luggages*, *chalks*, *furnitures*, etc.

2.   *use to* can be used with present tense meaning to indicate habitual activity:

I use to go shopping on Mondays   'I usually go shopping on Mondays'

3.   *Would* is often used rather than *will*:

We hope you would come tomorrow

4.   Again as in other non-native varieties, *is it?/isn't it?* are used as invariable tags:

He is going to buy a car, isn't it?

5.   Another interrogative tag which is typical of SingEng is *can or not?*:

She wants to go, can or not?   'Can she go (or not)?'

6.   The indefinite article is used less frequently than in native varieties of English:

He is teacher

7.   A number of discourse particles not found in other varieties of English, some of them derived from Chinese, are used in functions which in native varieties are signalled by intonation and/or syntactic devices. For example, *la* or *lah* is a particle signifying informality, solidarity and emphasis:

Please la come to the party   'Please *do* come to the party'

7.4.3.   SingEng lexis

Characteristic SingEng lexis consists in the main of items borrowed from Malay and Hokkien Chinese and of English words which have been semantically or grammatically extended.

chope	'to reserve'
koon	'sleep'
makan	'to eat, food'
tolong	'help'

alphabet	'letter' (of the alphabet)
hardwork	'hard work'
take	'to (like to) eat or drink'

7.5. English in the Philippines

The Philippines were a Spanish colony from 1521 until 1898, when they became an American colony. They became an independent nation in 1946. The indigenous languages, of which there are about 90, are members of the Austronesian language family. The official languages are Pilipino (a form of Tagalog) and English.

7.5.1. The pronunciation of PhilEng

1.   Unlike most of the non-native varieties of English in the British Commonwealth countries, but like most forms of USEng, Philippino English (PhilEng) is rhotic. Phonetically, /r/ is a flap, and not a continuant, as in USEng.
2.   PhilEng is syllable-timed (see 6.5.(7)).
3.   The voiced fricatives /z/ and /ž/ are generally lacking, being replaced by /s/ and /š/.
4.   /θ/ and /ð/ are often merged with /t/ and /d/, respectively.
5.   One possible vowel system is illustrated in Table 7.4. Notice the following points:

(a) /ɪ/ and /i/ are generally not distinct: *bit, beat* /bit/
(b) /ʊ/ and /u/ are generally not distinct: *pull, pool* /pul/
(c) /æ/ and /ɑ/ are generally not distinct: *cat, cot* /kɑt/
(d) /ɔ/ and /ou/ are generally not distinct: *caught, coat* /kot/.

Table 7.4.   The vowels of PhilEng

/i/	*bid, bee*
/e/	*bay*
/ɛ/	*bed*
/a/	*bad, pot, father*
/ɔ/	*putt*
/o/	*boat, paw*
/u/	*put, boot*
/ai/	*buy*
/oi/	*boy*
/au/	*bout*

7.5.2.   PhilEng grammar

1.   PhilEng, except in the most careful styles, tends to lack third-person -*s* on present-tense verb forms.

2.   The indefinite article is used less frequently than in native varieties of English:

He is teacher

3.   Verbs which in native varieties of English require an object or a complement may occur without one:

I don't like

4.   Pluperfect verb forms may be used where native speakers would expect a present perfect form:

He had already left   'He has already left'

7.5.3.   PhilEng lexis

Characteristically PhilEng lexis includes items borrowed from Spanish as well as from Tagalog and other indigenous languages:

from Spanish:
asalto	'surprise party'
estafa	'fraud'
querida	'girlfriend'

from indigenous languages:
boondock	'mountain'
carabao	'water buffalo'
kundiman	'love song'

Glossary

affricate   consonant characterized by the gradual release of air after a complete closure.

allophone   a particle realization (pronunciation) of a *phoneme* (vid.).

alveolar   consonant produced by the tip or blade of the tongue touching the alveolar ridge (the ridge behind the upper teeth).

anaphoric   referring back to some previous word(s) or meaning.

apical   manner of articulation of a consonant using the tip of the tongue.

approximant   consonant produced by two articulatory organs approaching each other without causing audible friction.

aspect   the marking on the verb or auxiliary indicating duration or completion of activity: e.g. progressive aspect (*-ing*) and perfective aspect (*have* + tense + participal).

aspirated   manner of articulation of a consonant whereby an audible rush of air accompanies the production of the consonant.

causative   a verb or clause expressing causation.

clefting   the grammatical process of focusing on an item by moving it to the front of its clause and preceding it by *it is/was/etc.*: e.g. *John bought a bicycle* can be clefted as *It was John who bought a bicycle* or *It was a bicycle that John bought.*

collocation   refers to words that habitually co-occur.

complement   in general, all elements of the predicate other than the verb.

continuant   a consonant produced by incomplete closure of the vocal tract.

copula   a stative verb which links or equates the subject and *complement* (vid.), e.g. *be.*

coreferential   refers to two words that have the same reference.

count noun   a noun whose referent is seen as a discrete, countable entity (opposite of *mass noun*, vid.); it can occur with an article and has a plural form.

creole   a *pidgin* language (vid.) which has acquired native speakers.

dark l   an *l* produced with *velarized* articulation (vid.).

deverbal noun   a noun derived from a verb.

diacritic   a mark added to a letter or symbol indicating a change in its usual pronunciation.

ellipsis   the omission of part of a sentence's structure which is recoverable from context.

epistemic   refers to a *modal* (vid.) which asserts that a proposition is known or believed to be true.

existential   refers to the use of *there* (*is*) to express existence (as opposed to location).

flap   manner of articulation (here of *d* and *r*) whereby the tip of the tongue makes a single rapid contact with the *alveolar* ridge.

fricative   consonant produced by two articulatory organs coming close enough together to cause audible friction.

glottalized   manner of articulation whereby the glottis (opening between the vocal cords) is constricted.

homophones   words with the same pronunciation but different meaning.

intervocalic   occurring between two vowels.

lateral   manner of articulation whereby air escapes around the sides of a closure, as in /l/.

lingua franca   a language used as a means of communication by speakers who do not have a native language in common.

mass noun   a noun whose referent is seen as being non-discrete, having no natural bounds (e.g. *air, happiness*); it cannot occur with an article and does not have a plural form.

modal   refers to auxiliaries used to express speaker attitudes to the proposition (e.g. obligation, certainty, possibility).

morpheme   minimal unit of meaning, used in the composition of words.

neutralization   the loss of distinction between two *phonemes* in a particular linguistic environment.

palatalized   manner of articulation whereby the blade of the tongue approaches or touches the hard palate.

partitive phrase   a phrase usually of the form $noun_1 + of + noun_2$ with the approximate meaning 'UNIT of ENTITY': e.g. *loaf of bread*.

periphrastic   using separate words rather than inflections to express some grammatical relationship.

phoneme   minimal distinctive unit of sound (the substitution in a word of one phoneme for another causes a change in meaning).

pidgin   a linguistically simplified, mixed and restricted language used in limited contact situations between people who have no common language.

plosive   consonant characterized by complete closure of the vocal tract followed by the sudden release of air.

quantifier   a word expressing quantity.

resumptive pronoun   a pronoun which marks the place of a noun that has been moved elsewhere in the sentence.

retroflex   manner of articulation whereby the tip of the tongue is curled back behind the *alveolar* ridge.

semi-auxiliary   words which have some properties of auxiliaries and some of verbs.

stative verb   a verb which denotes a state of being, relational process or perceptual process rather than an action.

subordinator   a conjunction which introduces a subordinate, or dependent, clause.

syllabic consonant   a consonant that can occur alone to form a syllable, as /n/ in *button*.

tag question   a question consisting of an auxiliary and pronoun attached to the end of a statement.

velarized   manner of articulation whereby the back of the tongue approaches the velum (soft palate).

voicing   refers to the vibration of the vocal cords: *voiced* sounds are produced with the vocal cords vibrating, while *voiceless* sounds are produced without them vibrating.

For further explication of these and other linguistic terms, the reader is referred to David Crystal's *A Dictionary of Linguistics and Phonetics*, Oxford: Blackwell, 1991 and to Peter Trudgill's *Introducing Language and Society*, London: Penguin, 1992.

Selected references and further reading

The journals *English Word Wide* (Amsterdam: Benjamins) and *World Englishes* (Oxford: Pergamon) are highly recommended.

Aitken, A. and McArthur, T. 1979: *Languages of Scotland*. Edinburgh: Chambers.
Allen, H. and Underwood, G. 1971: *Readings in American Dialectology*. New York, NY: Appleton-Century-Crofts.
Alleyne, M. C. 1980: *Comparative Afro-American: An Historical-Comparative Study of English-based Afro-American Dialects of the New World*. Ann Arbor, MI: Karoma.
Avis, W. S., Crate, C., Drysdale, P., Leechman, D., Scargill, M. H. and Lovell, C. O. 1967: *A Dictionary of Canadianisms on Historical Principles*. Toronto: W. J. Gage.
Bähr, D. 1974: *Standard Englisch und seine Geographischen Varianten*. Munich: Wilhelm Fink.
Bailey, R. W. and Görlach, M. 1982: *English as a World Language*. Ann Arbor, MI: University of Michigan Press.
Baker, S. J. 1966: *The Australian Language*. 2nd edition. Sydney: Curranan.
Baugh, A. C. and Cable, T. 1993: *A History of the English Language*. 4th edition. London: Routledge.
Bell, A. and Holmes, J. (eds) 1990: *New Zealand Ways of Speaking English*. Clevedon: Multilingual Matters.
Carver, C. M. 1987: *American Regional Dialects: A Word Geography*. Ann Arbor, MI: University of Michigan Press.
Cassidy, F. and Le Page, R. 1980: *Dictionary of Jamaican English*. Cambridge: CUP.
Chambers, J. K. 1975: *Canadian English: Origins and Structures*. London: Methuen.
Chambers, J. K. (ed.) 1979: *The Languages of Canada*. Paris: Didier.
Cheshire, J. (ed.) 1991: *English Around the World: Sociolinguistic Perspectives*. Cambridge: CUP.

Dillard, J. 1972: *Black English*. New York, NY: Random House.

Dillard, J. 1992: *A History of American English*. London: Longman.

Foster, B. 1968: *The Changing English Language*. London: Macmillan.

Francis, N. 1958: *The Structure of American English*. New York, NY: Ronald Press.

Gimson, A. C. 1990: *An Introduction to the Pronunciation of English*. 4th edition. London: Edward Arnold.

Gordon, E. and Deverson, T. 1985: *New Zealand English: An Introduction to New Zealand Speech and Usage*. Auckland: Heinemann.

Görlach, M. 1991: *Englishes: Studies in Varieties of English*. Amsterdam: Benjamins.

Harris, J., Little, D. and Singleton, D. 1986: *Perspectives on the English Language in Ireland*. Dublin: Trinity College.

Holm, J. (ed.) 1983: *Central American English*. Heidelberg: Groos.

Holm, J. and Shilling, A. 1982: *Dictionary of Bahamian English*. Cold Spring, NY: Lexik House.

Hughes, A. and Trudgill, P. 1987: *English Accents and Dialects: An Introduction to Social and Regional Varieties of British English*. 2nd edition. London: Edward Arnold.

Kachru, B. 1982: *Other Tongue: English in Non-Native Contexts*. Cambridge: CUP.

Kreidler, C. W. 1989: *The Pronunciation of English*. Oxford: Blackwell.

Lanham, L. 1967: *The Pronunciation of South African English*. Cape Town: Balkema.

Lanham, L. and Macdonald, C. 1979: *The Standard in South African English and its Social History*. Heidelberg: Groos.

Le Page, R. and De Camp, D. 1960: *Jamaican Creole*. London: Macmillan.

Mazzon, G. 1992: *L'Inglese di Malta*. Naples: Liguori.

McArthur, T. (ed.) 1992: *The Oxford Companion to the English Language*. Oxford: OUP.

McCrum, R., Cran, W. and MacNeil, R. 1986: *The Story of English*. London: Faber and Faber.

Mitchell, A. G. and Delbridge, A. 1965: *The Pronunciation of English in Australia*. Sydney: Angus and Robertson.

Nihalani, P., Tongue, R. K. and Hosali, P. 1979: *Indian and British English: A Handbook of Usage and Pronunciation*. Oxford: OUP.

O'Muirithe, D. (ed.) 1977: *The English Language in Ireland*. Cork: Mercier.

Orkin, M. M. 1970: *Speaking Canadian English*. Toronto: General.

Paddock, H. J. (ed.) 1982: *Languages in Newfoundland and Labrador*. 2nd edition. St Johns: Memorial University.

Platt, J. and Weber, H. 1980: *English in Singapore and Malaysia*. Oxford: OUP.

Platt, J., Weber, H. and Ho, M. L. 1984: *The New Englishes*. London: Routledge & Kegan Paul.

Pride, J. 1982: *New Englishes*. Rowley, MA: Newbury House.

Pyles, T. 1971: *The Origins and Development of the English Language*. 2nd edition. New York, NY: Harcourt Brace Jovanovich.

Ramson, W. 1970: *English Transported*. Canberra: ANU Press.

Schmied, J. 1991: *English in Africa*. London: Longman.

Shuy, R. W. 1967: *Discovering American Dialects*. Champaign, IL: NCTE.

Spencer, J. 1971: *The English Language in West Africa*. London: Longman.

Story, G., Kirwin, W. and Widdowson, J. 1982: *Dictionary of Newfoundland English*. Toronto: University of Toronto Press.

Strang, B. M. H. 1970: *A History of English*. London: Methuen.

Strevens, P. 1972: *British and American English*. London: Collier-Macmillan.

Švejcer, A. 1978: *Standard English in the United States and England*. The Hague: Mouton.

Todd, L. 1984: *Modern Englishes: Pidgins and Creoles*. Oxford: Blackwell.

Turner, G. 1966: *The English Language in Australia and New Zealand*. Harmondsworth: Longman.

Wells, J. C. 1982: *Accents of English: Vols 1, 2 and 3*. Cambridge: CUP.

Williamson, J. and Burke, V. 1971: *A Various Language*. New York, NY: Holt, Rinehart and Winston.

The recording

1. RP: Table 2.1, page 10
    RP: The reading passage

2. Australian English: Table 2.3, page 18
    Australian English: The reading passage

3. New Zealand English: Table 2.4, page 26
    New Zealand English: The reading passage

4. South African English: Table 2.5, page 30
    South African English: The reading passage

5. Welsh English: Table 2.5, page 30
    Welsh English: The reading passage

6(a). US English (Eastern): Table 3.1, page 38
       US English (Eastern): The reading passage

6(b). US English (Mid-Western): Table 3.1, page 38
       US English (Mid-Western): The reading passage

7. Canadian English: Table 3.1, page 38
    Canadian English: The reading passage

8. Scottish English: Table 5.1, page 95
    Scottish English: The reading passage

9. Northern Irish English: Table 5.1, page 95
    Northern Irish English: The reading passage

10. Southern Irish English: Table 5.2, page 104
     Southern Irish English: The reading passage

11. West Indian English: Table 2.1, page 10
     West Indian English: The reading passage

12. West African English: Table 2.1, page 10
     West African English: The reading passage

13. Indian English: Table 2.1, page 10
     Indian English: The reading passage

Notes

The RP speaker demonstrates the features more typical of younger RP speakers. See especially points 1 to 4 in section 2.1.1.

The West Indian speaker is from the island of Dominica.

The West African speaker is from Ghana and is a native speaker of Twi.

The Indian speaker is a native speaker of Tamil, a southern Indian language.

The same reading passage is used for all the varieties in the recording in order to facilitate comparison. Some speakers have made minor changes in the text to conform to the norms of their particular variety. All speakers on the tape are university or college educated.

The reading passage

(From Trudgill, P. 1975: *Accent, Dialect and the School*, pages 15–16. London: Edward Arnold.)

As a language changes, it may well change in different ways in different places. No one who speaks a particular language can remain in close contact with *all* the other speakers of that language. Social and geographical barriers to communication as well as sheer distance mean that a change that starts among speakers in one particular locality will probably spread only to other areas with which these speakers are in close contact. This is what has happened over the centuries in the case of the languages we now call English and German. Two thousand years ago the Germanic peoples living in what is now, for the most part, Germany could understand one another perfectly well. However, when many of them migrated to England they did not remain in close contact with those who stayed behind. The result, to simplify somewhat, was that different linguistic changes took place in the two areas independently so that today English and German, while clearly related languages, are not mutually intelligible. There was presumably a certain amount of inevitability about this process, since speakers usually need to remain intelligible only to those people they normally communicate with, and, until quite recently, close and frequent communication between England and Germany was not possible. But this also means that the same kind of process is unlikely to be repeated in such an extreme form in the case of different variants of modern English. American and British English have been geographically separated, and diverging linguistically, for 300 years or so, but the divergence is not very great because of the density of the communication between the two speech communities, particularly since the advent of modern transport and communication facilities. In other words, linguistic change in English will continue, but it is very unlikely indeed (barring prolonged world-wide catastrophes) that this will lead to a decrease in the mutual intelligibility of different varieties of English. That is, it is not legitimate to argue that change in English is a bad thing because it will lead to a breakdown in communication. It will not—so long as all English speakers need and are able to keep in touch with each other.

In fact, if anything, the reverse is more likely, since change does not necessarily take place in a 'divergent' direction. Where two groups of speakers develop closer social contacts than they previously had, their language is quite likely to converge. This appears to have happened in Jamaica, where the language spoken today is much more like British English than it was 200 years ago.

And even where change is of the divergent type, it should not necessarily be assumed that this is a bad thing. From many points of view, of course, it is true that a large increase in linguistic diversity on a world-wide scale would be unfortunate. Particularly in the sphere of international politics, it is desirable that different peoples should be able to communicate as freely and accurately as possible. But at the same time it is also valid to argue that the maintenance of a certain number of linguistic barriers to communication is a good thing. These barriers, although penetrable, ensure the survival of different language communities. And the separation of the world's population into different groups speaking different languages helps the growth of cultural diversity, which in turn can lead to opportunities for the development of alternative modes of exploring possibilities for social, political and technological progress. A world where everyone spoke the same language could be a very dull and stagnant place.

Index